Consumerism

Other Books of Related Interest:

Opposing Viewpoints Series

Debt

The Federal Budget

The Middle Class

White Collar Crime

Current Controversies Series

Capitalism

Consumer Debt

The Global Economy

The U.S. Economy

At Issue Series

Does Outsourcing Harm America?

Should the Federal Government Bail Out Private Industry?

Teens and Credit

"Congress shall make
no law . . . abridging
the freedom of speech,
or of the press."

First Amendment to the U.S. Constitution

The basic foundation of our democracy is the First Amendment guarantee of freedom of expression. The Opposing Viewpoints Series is dedicated to the concept of this basic freedom and the idea that it is more important to practice it than to enshrine it.

OPPOSING
VIEWPOINTS®
SERIES

Consumerism

Roman Espejo, Book Editor

GREENHAVEN PRESS
A part of Gale, Cengage Learning

GALE
CENGAGE Learning™

Detroit • New York • San Francisco • New Haven, Conn • Waterville, Maine • London

GALE
CENGAGE Learning

Christine Nasso, *Publisher*
Elizabeth Des Chenes, *Managing Editor*

LIBRARY OF CONGRESS CATALOGING-IN-PUBLICATION DATA

Consumerism / Roman Espejo, editor.
    p. cm. -- (Opposing viewpoints)
    Includes bibliographical references and index.
    978-0-7377-4506-1 (hardcover)
    978-0-7377-4507-8 (pbk.)
    1. Consumption (Economics)--Juvenile literature. I. Espejo, Roman, 1977-
    HB801.C62824 2009
    339.4'7--dc22

                                                        2009026339

Contents

Chapter 4: Should Consumerism Be Rejected?

Why Consider
Opposing Viewpoints?

> "The only way in which a human being can make some approach to knowing the whole of a subject is by hearing what can be said about it by persons of every variety of opinion and studying all modes in which it can be looked at by every character of mind. No wise man ever acquired his wisdom in any mode but this."
>
> John Stuart Mill

In our media-intensive culture it is not difficult to find differing opinions. Thousands of newspapers and magazines and dozens of radio and television talk shows resound with differing points of view. The difficulty lies in deciding which opinion to agree with and which "experts" seem the most credible. The more inundated we become with differing opinions and claims, the more essential it is to hone critical reading and thinking skills to evaluate these ideas. Opposing Viewpoints books address this problem directly by presenting stimulating debates that can be used to enhance and teach these skills. The varied opinions contained in each book examine many different aspects of a single issue. While examining these conveniently edited opposing views, readers can develop critical thinking skills such as the ability to compare and contrast authors' credibility, facts, argumentation styles, use of persuasive techniques, and other stylistic tools. In short, the Opposing Viewpoints Series is an ideal way to attain the higher-level thinking and reading skills so essential in a culture of diverse and contradictory opinions.

In addition to providing a tool for critical thinking, Opposing Viewpoints books challenge readers to question their own strongly held opinions and assumptions. Most people form their opinions on the basis of upbringing, peer pressure, and personal, cultural, or professional bias. By reading carefully balanced opposing views, readers must directly confront new ideas as well as the opinions of those with whom they disagree. This is not to simplistically argue that everyone who reads opposing views will—or should—change his or her opinion. Instead, the series enhances readers' understanding of their own views by encouraging confrontation with opposing ideas. Careful examination of others' views can lead to the readers' understanding of the logical inconsistencies in their own opinions, perspective on why they hold an opinion, and the consideration of the possibility that their opinion requires further evaluation.

Evaluating Other Opinions

To ensure that this type of examination occurs, Opposing Viewpoints books present all types of opinions. Prominent spokespeople on different sides of each issue as well as well-known professionals from many disciplines challenge the reader. An additional goal of the series is to provide a forum for other, less known, or even unpopular viewpoints. The opinion of an ordinary person who has had to make the decision to cut off life support from a terminally ill relative, for example, may be just as valuable and provide just as much insight as a medical ethicist's professional opinion. The editors have two additional purposes in including these less known views. One, the editors encourage readers to respect others' opinions—even when not enhanced by professional credibility. It is only by reading or listening to and objectively evaluating others' ideas that one can determine whether they are worthy of consideration. Two, the inclusion of such viewpoints encourages the important critical thinking skill of objectively evaluating an author's credentials and bias. This evaluation will illuminate an author's reasons for taking a particular stance on an issue and will aid in readers' evaluation of the author's ideas.

It is our hope that these books will give readers a deeper understanding of the issues debated and an appreciation of the complexity of even seemingly simple issues when good and honest people disagree. This awareness is particularly important in a democratic society such as ours in which people enter into public debate to determine the common good. Those with whom one disagrees should not be regarded as enemies but rather as people whose views deserve careful examination and may shed light on one's own.

Thomas Jefferson once said that "difference of opinion leads to inquiry, and inquiry to truth." Jefferson, a broadly educated man, argued that "if a nation expects to be ignorant and free . . . it expects what never was and never will be." As individuals and as a nation, it is imperative that we consider the opinions of others and examine them with skill and discernment. The Opposing Viewpoints Series is intended to help readers achieve this goal.

David L. Bender and Bruno Leone,
Founders

Introduction

> "Consumer confidence doesn't only reflect current economic conditions but fuels future growth."
>
> —Rabea Ataya,
> Baty.com, August 21, 2007

> "The indexes of consumer confidence are not of significant value in forecasting consumer spending. In fact, in some cases, they make the forecasts significantly worse."
>
> —Dean Croushore,
> "Do Consumer Confidence Indexes
> Help Forecast Consumer Spending
> in Real Time?" January 2005

Consumer confidence is essentially what it sounds like: consumers' overall outlook on the economy, incomes, and personal finances. It is directly linked to spending—the more people buy, the more fiscally confident they purportedly are. The term was made popular by John Maynard Keynes, a twentieth-century British economist. Keynes had coined the phrase "animal spirits" to describe consumer confidence in his 1936 book *The General Theory of Employment, Interest, and Money*. "Most, probably, of our decisions to do something positive, the full consequences of which will be drawn out over many days to come, can only be taken as the result of animal spirits—a spontaneous urge to action rather than inaction, and not as the outcome of a weighted average of quantitative benefits multiplied by quantitative probabilities." Within Keynes's framework, emotional fluctuations rather than rational thinking influence consumer confidence, affecting patterns of spending, saving, splurging, and hoarding.

In the United States, consumer confidence has been officially measured with The Conference Board Consumer Confidence Index (CCI) since 1967. The Conference Board, a business organization based in New York City, provides the CCI each month, relying on a survey of five thousand American households that gathers opinions on the current business conditions and expectations of employment and income. Professionals in the financial sector often refer to the CCI for a snapshot of consumption and the economy.

According to financial modeling consultant Ryan Barnes, the strengths of the index are that it is "one of few indicators that reaches out to average households" and "has historically been a good predictor of consumer spending and, therefore, the gross domestic product."[i] Barnes adds, however, that the CCI is subject to interpretation. "It is a highly subjective survey, and the results should be interpreted as such," he says. "People can grab onto a small situation that garners a lot of mainstream press, such as gas prices. . ."[ii] Nonetheless, other experts are skeptical of the CCI and the concept of consumer confidence itself. Gary North, author of *Mises on Money*, maintains, "Today, we read reports about the rise and fall of consumer confidence. But consumer confidence or lack thereof is placed in an economy in which discretionary spending is so marginal as to be almost irrelevant."[iii] Moreover, North insists that Keynes's economic theory is flawed: "[H]e thinks that immediate consumption drives the economy. Anything that threatens to reduce immediate consumption therefore threatens the economy. When people stop buying consumer goods on credit, this worries the Keynesian economist. When they use part of their income to pay off existing debt, this terrifies the Keynesian economist."[iv]

i. Investopedia, accessed June 2009
ii. Investopedia, accessed June 2009
iii. LewRockwell.com, August 5, 2003
iv. LewRockwell.com, August 5, 2003

Though it has its detractors, consumer confidence is one of several ways economists and analysts attempt to determine the fiscal state of America and create financial policies. For instance, a few critics of president Barack Obama's $900 billion stimulus package disparage it as "Keynesian," while others are faithful such aid will place American consumers—and the economy—back on track. *Opposing Viewpoints: Consumerism* addresses other issues surrounding consumption in the following chapters: "What Is the Impact of Consumerism?" "What Facilitates Consumerism?" "Is Consumerism a Problem?" and "Should Consumerism Be Rejected?" The breadth of views presented in the anthology underlines consumer phenomena as a polarizing feature of post-industrial society.

CHAPTER 1

What Is the Impact of Consumerism?

Chapter Preface

American sociologist Thorstein Veblen coined the term "conspicuous consumption" in *The Theory of the Leisure Class* to describe visible, costly spending on enjoyment and luxury. Published in 1899, the book was a critique of the impacts of the Industrial Revolution, particularly the flush of new wealth among an emerging social group. "During the earlier stages of economic development," wrote Veblen, "consumption of goods without stint, especially consumption of the better grades of goods—ideally all consumption in excess of the subsistence minimum—pertains normally to the leisure class." Rather than a sign of prosperity, he saw such activity as overindulgent and burdensome. "Under the requirement of the conspicuous consumption of goods, the apparatus of living has grown so elaborate and cumbrous, in the way of dwellings, furniture, bric-a-brac, wardrobe, and meals that the consumers of these things cannot make way with them in the required manner without help," Veblen asserted. But his most striking claim in *The Theory of the Leisure Class* was that conspicuous consumption was predatory behavior, wherein the acquisition of goods was a barbaric display of power and bid for dominance. "Tangible evidence of prowess—trophies—finds a place as an essential feature of the paraphernalia of life. Booty, trophies of the chase or of the raid, come to be prized as evidence of preeminent force. Aggression becomes the accredited form of action, and booty serves as 'prima facie' [at first view] evidence of successful aggression."

The Theory of the Leisure Class is regarded as the first major analysis of consumerism as a social phenomenon. Other concepts in the vein of Veblen's have followed suit, such as "keeping up with the Joneses," "status symbol," and "affluenza." In the following chapter, the authors present contemporary views on the social and economic implications of what people buy.

> "Since Americans are consuming enthu-
> siastically, they must be optimistic
> about the future."

Consumption Is Linked to Economic Well-Being

Kevin A. Hassett and Aparna Mathur

In the following viewpoint, Kevin A. Hassett and Aparna Mathur maintain that consumption is a reliable measure of income. In particular, Hasset and Mathur assert that the growth rate of consumption among the middle class has increased between 2000 and 2005—a show of economic prosperity that takes into consideration taxation, income fluctuation, and other complex variables. And while skeptics propose that the rise in middle-class spending is linked to increased credit card debt and money withdrawn from inflated housing wealth, the authors assert that trends in consumer behavior indicate that people cut back on spending and save more according to the economic outlook. Hassett is director of economic policy studies at the American Enterprise Institute, where Mathur is a research fellow.

As you read, consider the following questions:

1. In the authors' opinion, how are Republicans portrayed?

2. How do the authors respond to the statistic that incomes increased 0.6 percent per year between 2000 and 2006?

3. How do Hassett and Mathur support their argument that economic growth benefits the middle class, not just the wealthy?

When George W. Bush took office in January 2001, the economy was producing roughly $10 trillion worth of output annually. This year [2006], it looks like production will be in the neighborhood of $13.5 trillion. If we think of our nation's GDP [gross domestic product] as analogous to an individual's income, then that lucky fellow has seen his income increase over the past six years by about 35 percent. A person making $100,000 who saw the same increase in his income would now be making $135,000.

So are we better off today than we were in 2001? Despite the healthy growth, this is not a trivial question—for two reasons. First, it might be that the extra 35 percent in current-dollar national income does not go as far with today's prices. Second, it might be that the income went only to a few people, and that most people did not share in the growth.

Many recent articles have in fact suggested that, despite the great economic numbers, things are terrible. For example, [economist] Paul Krugman claimed in *The New York Times* that "the lion's share of the benefits from recent economic growth has gone to a small, wealthy minority, while most Americans were worse off in 2005 than they were in 2000. . . . The rich are getting richer, but most working Americans are losing ground."

Behind these ominous trends appears to be some kind of conspiracy of the privileged. Republicans are against the little guy, and use the power of the presidency to protect and enable the big businesses that feed on him. In this, modern-day populists are just rehashing age-old Marxist propaganda. As a consequence of the concentration of power and wealth among the bourgeoisie, [socialists Karl] Marx and [Frederick] Engels argued, workers' wages would be stuck at subsistence levels, for "no sooner has the labourer received his wages in cash, for the moment escaping exploitation by the manufacturer, then he is set upon by the other portions of the bourgeoisie—the landlord, the shopkeeper, the pawnbroker, etc." Substitute Wal-Mart in there someplace, and you are at a meeting with [former chairman of the Democratic National Committee] Howard Dean.

Today, populists argue that rising costs of health care and energy combined with falling wages are taking a terrible toll on the average American worker and putting a squeeze on the working middle class. Growth no longer helps them. You've probably heard that story so often you accept it as gospel truth. But the story is poppycock. When you look at the most accurate measures of how the middle class is doing, the answer is that things are good, maybe even terrific.

The Flawed Arguments

But before we look at the right answer, let's look at the flawed arguments.

Are workers taking home less pay than before? Some measures of wages suggest that they have disappointed in recent years. In order to get this spin, you generally have to exclude benefits. For example, between 2000 and 2006 real wages—which exclude benefits—increased 0.6 percent per year; but real hourly compensation, which includes benefits, increased 1.3 percent per year. So if you think benefits are a good thing, then you should believe that workers are moving ahead. If you do not believe so, it might help if you started calling them something else.

Increasing Wealth in the United States

There are 1.2 million households with a net worth of over $5 million, up from 300,000 in 1983. Real household income for the top 20% of households is up 70% in the last 20 years. And 215 million people will be over 50 by 2010. As a result, $12 trillion in inheritance will change hands in the next 20 years. The top 5% are richer. In the early 1980s they accounted for 16% of the income earned. Today they account for 27%. The rich are definitely getting richer.

Alf Nucifora with Greg Furman,
"Why the Luxury Market Continues to Soar,"
September 23, 2005. www.nucifora.com.

But even if we rely on the wage numbers that include benefits, the numbers still understate how fast the average American is moving ahead. First, wage measures usually exclude taxes and transfers—but taxes have declined enormously, especially for middle-class families with small children. That makes a difference. And second, these measures adjust for inflation—which can be misleading in our present circumstances. Inflation has been surprisingly high in recent years, owing chiefly to sharp increases in energy prices; these increases likely moved consumers to change their behavior, trading in the Hummer for a Prius. Deflation can overcorrect for price changes if the model does not allow for changes in consumer behavior. (If I ate 80 apples last year, and the price of apples increased this year to a million dollars, my welfare would not go way down; I would just switch to oranges.)

Consumption as a Measure for How Well Off People Are

But there's another way to measure how people are doing: consumption. One benefit of looking at consumption is that it accounts for all of the other complicated things that are going on with income, such as taxes or black-market income. It also accounts for fluctuation of income over time. Consumption is generally smoothed over time by people to match their expected income. A person's consumption provides a much more accurate read on how he's doing than does his before-tax income.

So how have the consumption numbers been doing? Just as GDP has been rising, so has aggregate consumption. Between 2001 and the second quarter of this year [2006], the consumption of Americans grew 17.24 percent.

But the populists' claims are specifically about "the middle class." To find out how *they* are doing, we need to dig deeper into the source data. The Department of Labor's Consumer Expenditure Survey provides detailed consumption data on a cross section of Americans; we can use this to estimate how much of our aggregate consumption went to each income group in recent years.

These data reveal that the middle class has been doing pretty well for itself. Breaking the income distribution up into five quintiles, we tracked the consumption experience of the middle quintile (or middle class) in recent years. The data tell a striking story: Consumption has increased solidly for the middle class. Paul Krugman has claimed that people are worse off today than they were in 2000 because "once you adjust for inflation, you find that the income of a typical household headed by a college graduate was lower in 2005 than in 2000." But if the measure of *income* he chooses is a good measure of welfare, then *consumption* should stagnate as well—and, in fact, the opposite has happened. Adjusting for inflation, we estimate that the real growth rate of consumption for the middle class between 2000 and 2005 was about 7.5 percent. So the welfare of the middle is improving, and unambiguously. There is nothing to debate. The strong economy is lifting all boats.

The data also reject the view that we are evolving toward an economy that is less friendly toward the middle class. Indeed, the rate at which consumption by the middle class is increasing has accelerated in recent years. The average annual consumption growth for the middle class was less than 1 percent in the period from 1990 to 1994, rose to 1.5 percent in the period from 1995 to 1999, and jumped to more than 2 percent in the period from 2000 to 2005. The middle class is even doing better than the upper crust: The growth of their consumption expenditures exceeded the growth rate in the highest income category between 2000 and 2005. Consumption is becoming more equal across these income classes.

A pessimist might argue that the middle class has been able to increase its consumption because it took money out of its inflated housing wealth, or loaded up on credit card debt. Such moves might presage a big drop in consumption in the next few years. Perhaps, but this story seems exactly backward to us. Economists have studied individual consumption behavior for many years, and one thing they have indisputably learned is that people adjust when times are troubling. When individuals are fearful about the future, they reduce their consumption and increase their saving. This gives them a buffer stock of wealth to tide them over if things get rough. Since Americans are consuming enthusiastically, they must be optimistic about the future.

Consumption is a measure of what people use and eat. It has increased sharply in recent years, revealing the flawed income statistics as woefully inadequate measures of well-being. The proof is, we believe, in the pudding: The times are better than they used to be. The middle class is flourishing and optimistic.

| *"Conspicuous consumption, this research suggests, is not an unambiguous signal of personal affluence."*

Consumption Is Not an Indicator of Economic Well-Being

Virginia Postrel

In the following viewpoint, Virginia Postrel argues that conspicuous consumption—particularly of luxury goods—is not a signal of affluence. Instead, she suggests that it is a sign of belonging to a poorer group and is intended to fend off the negative perceptions of being poor. Postrel claims that research has revealed that African American families, who are poorer on average, spent 25 percent more on highly visible goods such as jewelry, cars, and apparel than whites with similar family sizes and incomes. According to the author, as a group becomes richer, luxury becomes less about status and more about personal enjoyment. Postrel is a columnist for Atlantic *and author of* The Substance of Style: How the Rise of Aesthetic Value Is Remaking Commerce, Culture, and Consciousness.

As you read, consider the following questions:

1. What reasons does the author provide that may explain African Americans' different spending patterns?

2. According to the author, how does conspicuous consumption to fend off the impression of poverty apply to whites?

3. As stated by Postrel, what do affluent consumers focus on?

About seven years ago [in 2001], University of Chicago economists Kerwin Kofi Charles and Erik Hurst were researching the "wealth gap" between black and white Americans when they noticed something striking. African Americans not only had less wealth than whites with similar incomes, they also had significantly more of their assets tied up in cars. The statistic fit a stereotype reinforced by countless bling-filled hip-hop videos: that African Americans spend a lot on cars, clothes, and jewelry—highly visible goods that tell the world the owner has money.

But do they really? And, if so, why?

The two economists, along with Nikolai Roussanov of the University of Pennsylvania, have now attacked those questions. What they found not only provides insight into the economic differences between racial groups, it challenges common assumptions about luxury. Conspicuous consumption, this research suggests, is not an unambiguous signal of personal affluence. It's a sign of belonging to a relatively poor group. Visible luxury thus serves less to establish the owner's positive status as affluent than to fend off the negative perception that the owner is poor. The richer a society or peer group, the less important visible spending becomes.

On race, the folk wisdom turns out to be true. An African American family with the same income, family size, and other demographics as a white family will spend about 25 percent more of its income on jewelry, cars, personal care, and apparel. For the average black family, making about $40,000 a year, that amounts to $1,900 more a year than for a comparable white family. To make up the difference, African Americans spend much less on education, health care, entertainment, and home furnishings. (The same is true of Latinos.)

Of course, different ethnic groups could simply have different tastes. Maybe blacks just enjoy jewelry more than whites do. Maybe they buy costlier clothes to deter slights from racist salesclerks. Maybe they spend more on cars for historical reasons, because of the freedom auto travel gave African Americans during the days of segregated trains and buses. Maybe they just aren't that interested in private colleges or big-screen TVs. Or maybe not. Economists hate unfalsifiable tautologies [needless repetition without adding useful information about an idea] about differing tastes. They want stories that could apply to anyone.

So the researchers went back to Thorstein Veblen, who coined the term *conspicuous consumption*. Writing in the much poorer world of 1899, Veblen argued that people spent lavishly on visible goods to prove that they were prosperous. "The motive is emulation—the stimulus of an invidious [causing envy] comparison which prompts us to outdo those with whom we are in the habit of classing ourselves," he wrote. Along these lines, the economists hypothesized that visible consumption lets individuals show strangers they aren't poor. Since strangers tend to lump people together by race, the lower your racial group's income, the more valuable it is to demonstrate your personal buying power.

To test this idea, the economists compared the spending patterns of people of the same race in different states—say, blacks in Alabama versus blacks in Massachusetts, or whites in South Carolina versus whites in California. Sure enough, all else being equal (including one's own income), an individual spent more of his income on visible goods as his racial group's

Consuming to Flaunt Success

Economists refer to items that we purchase in order to reveal our prosperity to others as wealth *signals*. But why use sneakers, as opposed to phonics toys, as a wealth signal? First off, for a signal to be effective, it needs to be easily observed by the people we're trying to impress. This includes not just those near and dear to us, but also the person we pass on the street, who sees our sneakers but would have a harder time inferring how much we're spending teaching our kids to read. For a wealth signal to be credible, it also needs to be hard to imitate—if everyone in your community can afford $150 sneakers, those Zoom Lebron IVs would lose their signal value.

Ray Fisman, "Cos and Effect,"
Slate, January 11, 2008.

income went down. African Americans don't necessarily have different tastes from whites. They're just poorer, on average. In places where blacks in general have more money, individual black people feel less pressure to prove their wealth.

The same is true for whites. Controlling for differences in housing costs, an increase of $10,000 in the mean income for white households—about like going from South Carolina to California—leads to a 13 percent decrease in spending on visible goods. "Take a $100,000-a-year person in Alabama and a $100,000 person in Boston," says Hurst. "The $100,000 person in Alabama does more visible consumption than the $100,000 person in Massachusetts." That's why a diamond-crusted Rolex screams "nouveau riche." It signals that the owner came from a poor group and has something to prove.

So this research has implications beyond race. It ought to apply to any peer group perceived by strangers. It suggests why emerging economies like Russia and China, despite their low average incomes, are such hot luxury markets today—and why 20th-century Texas, a relatively poor state, provided so many eager customers for Neiman Marcus. Rich people in poor places want to show off their wealth. And their less affluent counterparts feel pressure to fake it, at least in public. Nobody wants the stigma of being thought poor. Veblen was right.

But he was also wrong. Or at least his theory is out of date. Given that the richer your group, the less flashy spending you'll do, conspicuous consumption isn't a universal phenomenon. It's a development phase. It declines as countries, regions, or distinct groups get richer. "Bling rules in emerging economies still eager to travel the status-through-product consumption road," the market-research group Euromonitor recently noted, but luxury businesses "are becoming aware that bling isn't enough for growing numbers of consumers in developed economies." At some point, luxury becomes less a tool of public status competition and more a means to private pleasure.

In Veblen's day, the less affluent scrimped on their homes in order to keep up appearances in public. "The domestic life of most classes is relatively shabby, as compared with the éclat [ostentatious display] of that overt portion of their life that is carried on before the eyes of observers," Veblen wrote, noting that people therefore "habitually screen their private life from observation." By contrast, consider David Brooks's observation in *Bobos in Paradise* that, for today's educated elites,

> it's virtuous to spend $25,000 on your bathroom, but it's vulgar to spend $15,000 on a sound system and a wide-screen TV. It's decadent to spend $10,000 on an outdoor Jacuzzi, but if you're not spending twice that on an over-sized slate shower stall, it's a sign that you probably haven't learned to appreciate the simple rhythms of life.

Virtuous or vulgar, what all these items have in common is that they're invisible to strangers. Only your friends and family see them. Any status they confer applies only within the small group you invite to your home. And the snob appeal Brooks pokes fun at corresponds to the size of the audience. Many friends may see your Jacuzzi or media room, but unless you're on HGTV, only intimates will tour your master bathroom. A slate shower stall may make you feel rich, but it won't tell the world that you are. As peer groups get richer, the balance between private pleasure and publicly visible consumption shifts.

Russ Alan Prince and Lewis Schiff describe a similar pattern in their book *The Middle-Class Millionaire*, which analyzes the spending habits of the 8.4 million American households whose wealth is self-made and whose net worth, including their home equity, is between $1 million and $10 million. Aside from a penchant for fancy cars, these millionaires devote their luxury dollars mostly to goods and services outsiders can't see: concierge health care, home renovations, all sorts of personal coaches, and expensive family vacations. They focus less on impressing strangers and more on family- and self-improvement. Even when they invest in traditional luxuries like second homes, jets, or yachts, they prefer fractional ownership. "They're looking for ownership to be converted into a relationship rather than an asset they have to take care of," says Schiff. Their primary luxuries are time and attention.

The shift away from conspicuous consumption—from goods to services and experiences—can also make luxury more exclusive. Anyone with $6,000 can buy a limited-edition Bottega Veneta bag, an elaborately beaded Roberto Cavalli minidress, or a Cartier watch. Or, for the same sum, you can register for the TED [Technology, Entertainment, Design] conference. That $6,000 ticket entitles you to spend four days in California hearing short talks by brainy innovators, famous ([architect] Frank Gehry, [author] Amy Tan, [physicist] Brian Greene) and not-so-known. You get to mingle with smart, curious people, all of whom have $6,000 to spare. But to go to TED, you need more than cash. The conference directors have to deem you interesting enough to merit one of the 1,450 spots. It's the intellectual equivalent of a velvet rope.

As for goods, forget showing off. "If you want to live like a billionaire, buy a $12,000 bed," says a financial planner friend of mine. You can't park a mattress in your driveway, but it will last for decades and you can enjoy it every night.

| "*Corporate-driven consumerism is having massive psychological effects.*"

Consumerism May Be Linked to Mental and Emotional Problems

Tori DeAngelis

In the following viewpoint, Tori DeAngelis states that Americans today have more consumer goods than five decades ago, but they are not necessarily happier. According to DeAngelis, research reveals that compared with their grandparents, young Americans are slightly less happy and at much higher risk of depression and other psychological problems. In fact, individuals with strong materialistic values may have aspirations that lead to poorer well-being. Other researchers claim that avid consumers may also place unrealistic expectations on how much material wealth can improve their lives. Overall, the author concludes that consumer culture and its potential consequences are of increasing concern to psychologists. DeAngelis is a writer based in Syracuse, New York.

As you read, consider the following questions:

1. How are Americans today more affluent, as described by the author?

2. According to DeAngelis, what do researchers believe are the roots of materialistic values?

3. In one study, how did materialistic and prosocial values affect stress levels, as stated by the author?

Compared with Americans in 1957, today we own twice as many cars per person, eat out twice as often and enjoy endless other commodities that weren't around then—big-screen TVs, microwave ovens, SUVs and handheld wireless devices, to name a few. But are we any happier?

Certainly, happiness is difficult to pin down, let alone measure. But a recent literature review suggests we're no more contented than we were then—in fact, maybe less so.

"Compared with their grandparents, today's young adults have grown up with much more affluence, slightly less happiness and much greater risk of depression and assorted social pathology," notes Hope College psychologist David G. Myers, PhD, author of the article, which appeared in the *American Psychologist.* "Our becoming much better off over the last four decades has not been accompanied by one iota of increased subjective well-being."

These findings emerge at a time when the consumer culture has reached a fever pitch, comments Myers, also the author of "The American Paradox: Spiritual Hunger in an Age of Plenty."

So what does psychologists' research say about possible effects of this consumer culture on people's mental well-being? Based on the literature to date, it would be too simplistic to say that desire for material wealth unequivocally means discontent. Although the least materialistic people report the most life satisfaction, some studies indicate that materialists can be almost as contented if they've got the money and their acquisitive lifestyle doesn't conflict with more soul-satisfying pursuits. But for materialists with less money and other conflicting desires—a more common situation—unhappiness emerges, researchers are finding.

"There's a narrowing of the gap between materialists and nonmaterialists in life satisfaction as materialists' income rises," notes Edward Diener, PhD, a well-known researcher of subjective well-being and materialism at the University of Illinois at Urbana-Champaign. "So if you're poor, it's very bad to be a materialist; and if you're rich, it doesn't make you happier than nonmaterialists, but you almost catch up."

Why Are Materialists Unhappy?

As with all things psychological, the relationship between mental state and materialism is complex: Indeed, researchers are still trying to ascertain whether materialism stokes unhappiness, unhappiness fuels materialism, or both. Diener suggests that several factors may help explain the apparent toll of pursuit of wealth. In simple terms, a strong consumerist bent—what William Wordsworth in 1807 called "getting and spending"—can promote unhappiness because it takes time away from the things that can nurture happiness, including relationships with family and friends, research shows.

"It's not absolutely necessary that chasing after material wealth will interfere with your social life," Diener says. "But it can, and if it does, it probably has a net negative payoff in terms of life satisfaction and well-being."

People with strong materialistic values appear to have goal orientations that may lead to poorer well-being, adds Knox College psychologist Tim Kasser, PhD, who with Berkeley, Calif., psychotherapist Allen Kanner, PhD, co-edited a new APA book, *Psychology and Consumer Culture*, featuring experts' research and views on the links between consumerism, well-being and environmental and social factors.

In Kasser's own book, *The High Price of Materialism*, Kasser describes his and others' research showing that when people organize their lives around extrinsic goals such as product acquisition, they report greater unhappiness in relationships, poorer moods and more psychological problems. Kasser distinguishes extrinsic goals—which tend to focus on possessions, image, status and receiving rewards and praise—from intrinsic ones, which aim at outcomes like personal growth and community connection and are satisfying in and of themselves.

Relatedly, a not-yet-published study by University of Missouri social psychologist Marsha Richins, PhD, finds that materialists place unrealistically high expectations on what consumer goods can do for them in terms of relationships, autonomy and happiness.

"They think that having these things is going to change their lives in every possible way you can think of," she says. One man in Richins's study, for example, said he desperately wanted a swimming pool so he could improve his relationship with his moody 13-year-old daughter.

The Roots of Materialism

Given that we all experience the same consumeristic culture, why do some of us develop strongly materialistic values and others don't? A line of research suggests that insecurity—both financial and emotional—lies at the heart of consumeristic cravings. Indeed, it's not money per se, but the striving for it, that's linked to unhappiness, find Diener and others.

"Research suggests that when people grow up in unfortunate social situations—where they're not treated very nicely by their parents or when they experience poverty or even the threat of death," says Kasser, "they become more materialistic as a way to adapt."

A 1995 paper in *Developmental Psychology* by Kasser and colleagues was the first to demonstrate this. Teens who reported having higher materialistic attitudes tended to be poorer and to have less nurturing mothers than those with lower materialism scores, the team found. Similarly, a 1997 study in the *Journal of Consumer Research* headed up by Aric Rindfleisch, PhD, then a doctoral student at the University of Wisconsin-Madison and now an associate professor of marketing there, found that young people whose parents were undergoing or had undergone divorce or separation were more prone to developing materialistic values later in life than those from intact homes.

And in the first direct experimental test of the point, Kasser and University of Missouri social psychologist Kenneth Sheldon, PhD, reported in a 2000 article in *Psychological Science* that when provoked with thoughts of the most extreme uncertainty of them all—death—people reported more materialistic leanings.

More Money=Greater Happiness?

The ill effects of materialism appear subject to modification, other research finds. In a longitudinal study [involving repeated observation of a set of subjects over time], reported in the November 2003 issue of *Psychological Science*, psychologists Carol Nickerson, PhD, of the University of Illinois at Urbana-Champaign, Norbert Schwarz, PhD, of the University of Michigan, Diener, and Daniel Kahneman, PhD, of Princeton University, examined two linked data sets collected 19 years apart on 12,000 people who had attended elite colleges and universities in the 1970s—one drawn in 1976 when they were freshmen, the other in 1995.

On average, those who had initially expressed stronger financial aspirations reported lower life satisfaction two decades later than those expressing lower monetary desires. But as the income of the higher-aspiration participants rose, so did their reported life satisfaction, the team found.

How to Feel Wealthy

There are two ways to make people richer, reasoned [philosopher Jean-Jacques], Rousseau: to give them more money or to restrain their desires. Modern societies have succeeded spectacularly at the first option but, by continuously inflaming appetites, they have at the same time helped to negate a share of their most impressive achievements. The most effective way to feel wealthy may not be to try to make more money. It may be to distance ourselves—practically and emotionally—from anyone whom we consider to be our equal but who has become richer than ourselves. Rather than trying to become bigger fish, we could concentrate our energies on gathering around us smaller companions next to whom our own size will not trouble us.

Alain de Botton, "Part One: Causes: V: Expectation,"
Status Anxiety. *New York: Penguin Books, 2004, p. 62.*

James E. Burroughs, PhD, assistant professor of commerce at the University of Virginia's McIntire School of Commerce, and the University of Wisconsin's Rindfleisch conclude that the unhappiest materialists are those whose materialistic and higher-order values are most conflicted. In a 2002 paper in the *Journal of Consumer Research*, the team first gauged people's levels of stress, materialistic values and prosocial values in the domains of family, religion and community—in keeping with the theory of psychologist Shalom Schwartz, PhD, that some values unavoidably conflict with one another. Then in an experimental study, they ascertained the degree of conflict people felt when making a decision between the two value domains.

The unhappiest people were those with the most conflict—those who reported high prosocial *and* high materialistic values, says Burroughs. The other three groups—those low
in materialism and high in prosocial values, those low in
prosocial values and high in materialism, and those lukewarm
in both arenas—reported similar, but lower levels of life stress.

His findings square with those of others: that the differences in life satisfaction between more and less materialistic
people are relatively small, says Burroughs. And most researchers in the area agree that these values lie along a continuum,
he adds.

"Material things are neither bad nor good," Burroughs
comments. "It is the role and status they are accorded in one's
life that can be problematic. The key is to find a balance: to
appreciate what you have, but not at the expense of the things
that really matter—your family, community and spirituality."

The Bigger Picture

Even if some materialists swim through life with little distress,
however, consumerism carries larger costs that are worth worrying about, others say. "There are consequences of materialism that can affect the quality of other people's and other
species' lives," says Kasser.

To that end, he and others are beginning to study links between materialistic values and attitudes toward the environment, and to write about the way consumerism has come to
affect our collective psyche. Psychotherapist Kanner, who co-
edited *Psychology and Consumer Culture* with Kasser, cites examples as minor as parents who "outsource" parental activities
like driving their children to school and those as big as international corporations leading people in poor countries to
crave products they can ill afford.

Indeed, consumerism is an example of an area where psychology needs to stretch from its focus on the individual and
examine the wider impact of the phenomenon, Kanner believes.

"Corporate-driven consumerism is having massive psychological effects, not just on people, but on our planet as well," he says. "Too often, psychology over-individualizes social problems. In so doing, we end up blaming the victim, in this instance by locating materialism primarily in the person while ignoring the huge corporate culture that's invading so much of our lives."

"What we have here is plain old prejudice—against garish consumerism, especially of a kind indulged in by the
nouveaux riches—dressed up as a scientific study."

Consumerism Is Not Linked to Mental and Emotional Problems

Brendan O'Neill

*In the following viewpoint, Brendan O'Neill refutes scientific al-
legations that consumerism and materialistic desire are linked to
upswings of emotional distress and psychological disorders. He
counters the argument that people experience more stress in
highly capitalist countries, offering that citizens of countries
racked by poverty and unemployment also report high levels of
stress. O'Neill also challenges the perception that people today
are unhappier than in past eras, when hardship was commonplace and historic upheavals transformed daily life. Instead, he
believes that the spread of America's "therapy culture" has given
rise to the view that normal problems and emotions are "illnesses" that must be treated. O'Neill is editor of* spiked, *a political and cultural online magazine based in London, England.*

Brendan O'Neill, "When Ignorance Is Bliss," *New Statesman*, vol. 137, January 28, 2008,
p. 52(3). Copyright © 2008 New Statesman, Ltd. Reproduced by permission.

As you read, consider the following questions:

1. In O'Neill's view, how have socialist views of capitalism changed?

2. Which nations does the author state have been most affected by "therapy culture?"

3. What is O'Neill's opinion on the government prioritizing "well-being"?

In the 1980s there were champagne socialists, those Bollinger-swiggin[1] Thatcher-bashers[2] who cheered on the workers and sometimes handed wads of cash to the unions. Today we have the herbal-tea socialist. This new breed of lefty is more likely to be therapeutically minded and green-leaning, and to fret about capitalism "stressing out" the workers. The herbal-tea socialist wants to massage our minds rather than fund our fightbacks; he thinks we need therapy, not theory.

The most striking thing about herbal-tea socialism is its focus on the alleged evils of consumerism. Old Marxists quite admired the consumer society. [Socialist] Karl Marx himself praised its "charms" and "chatter", writing: "In spite of all his 'pious' speeches, [the capitalist] searches for means to spur [the workers] on to consumption, to give his wares new charms, to inspire them with new needs by constant chatter, etc. It is precisely this side of the relation of capital and labour which is an essential civilising moment." For Marxists, it was in the sphere of production, not consumption, that man was most degraded. It was there that he was exploited and alienated from his creative endeavours—and it was there that he had the power to change things. Only through overhauling production, Marxists argued, could man be made free.

1. Bollinger is a producer of sparkling wines from the champagne region of France.
2. Margaret Thatcher served as the British Prime Minister from 1979 to 1990. Along with Ronald Reagan, she founded a school of conservative politics that encouraged free markets and the spread of democracy.

Condemning Consumerism

Contrast that with herbal-tea socialism. Whether it's Buy Nothing Day campaigners hectoring the "sheep" of Oxford Street [a major area for shopping in London, England] into detoxing from shopping, or environmentalists claiming that our addiction to "stuff" (a disease some refer to as "stuff-itis") is making us mentally ill, the herbal-tea socialist is myopically [lacking long-term thinking] outraged by what we buy, rather than how exploited or un-free we are. Where Marx considered workers to be the gravediggers of capitalism, the herbal-tea socialist sees us as zombies of consumerism.

Herbal-tea socialism has a new bible in Oliver James's *The Selfish Capitalist*. Nothing better captures the snobbery and paternalism of the new anti-capitalism than James's tome. Dolled up to look like a fearless, searing critique of modern capitalist society, it is actually a deeply prejudicial, historically illiterate and conservative broadside against people's desire for material comfort and wealth.

James is a clinical child psychologist. In his last book, *Affluenza: How to Be Successful and Stay Sane*, he claimed to have uncovered a new virus. "Affluenza", he said, is brought on by the rampant materialism and cult of consumerism nurtured under "Blatcherism" (that's Blairism [Tony Blair] and Thatcherism combined). As we are encouraged to lust after stuff, to aspire to live the mock-Tudor lifestyle of a super-wealthy, blinged-up footballer's wife, we begin to neglect non-material matters such as friendships and family relations, argued James; we become emotionally distressed, destructively perfectionist, and discontented, sex-addicted and domineering to boot.

The Selfish Capitalist promises to trace the "origins of affluenza". One of James's central claims is that there is twice the prevalence of emotional distress or "mental illness" in English-speaking "selfish capitalist" nations there is in the "unselfish capitalist" nations of mainland western Europe. This suggests that materialism is driving us Brits mad, literally.

There are just a few problems with James's thesis. He never convincingly demonstrates that mental distress is higher in the "selfish capitalist" world than it is elsewhere. He shows no direct causal relationship between materialistic desire and levels of emotional distress. And the implications of his argument— where, in effect, the government is encouraged to manage our well-being—are so borderline Orwellian [evoking the works of George Orwell] that they make Blatcherism look almost progressive. Yes, "selfish capitalism" leaves us edgy and unfulfilled; but what we might refer to as the therapeutic socialism that James seems keen to instal would turn us into mental slaves.

James says that where 23 percent of people in "selfish capitalist" nations (the United States, Britain, Australia, Canada and New Zealand) have suffered emotional distress in the recent period, only 11.5 percent of people in "unselfish capitalist" nations (France, the Netherlands, Belgium, Spain, Germany, Italy and Japan) have been distressed. This finding is the foundation on which he builds his thesis about the perils of life in a neoliberal society. Yet James has to play the role of research contortionist to arrive at the claim that people in the selfish capitalist sphere are twice as likely to be unhappy.

He kicks off by citing the findings of a study by the World Health Organization [WHO] into the "percentage of the population [in different countries] that has suffered a mental distress in the past 12 months". Of the 15 countries probed to date, the US and New Zealand come [out on] top: 26.4 percent of Americans and 20.7 percent of New Zealanders claim to have "suffered a mental distress" recently. Must be that pesky selfish capitalism they're forced to live under. But what's this? Ukraine, better known for its poverty and unemployment than for any epidemic of Posh-and-Becks-style [British celebrity couple Victoria and David Beckham] materialism, comes third in the WHO's "league of woe": 20.5 percent of

Ukrainians say they have recently suffered mental distress. Colombia (17.8 percent) and Lebanon (16.9 percent), hardly nations in which disposable income is sloshing around, come fifth and sixth.

Most strikingly, Shanghai is at the bottom of the WHO's list of screwed-up territories: only 4.3 percent of its residents have recently been seriously stressed. Yet it is hard to think of a country where naked ambition and the desire for stuff is stronger than China right now, where two coal-fired power stations are erected every week, gleaming new skyscrapers poke holes in the clouds, and tens of thousands are abandoning back-breaking tasks in the countryside to get proper jobs (and TVs and cars) in the city.

Neat and Tidy Explanations

If "selfish capitalism" and its sidekick rampant consumerism provoke mental distress, why aren't the Chinese suffering but people in Colombia are? James has some neat and tidy explanations. Colombia and Lebanon might be distressed as a result of "social unrest and civil war"; Ukraine is probably emotionally under the weather as a result of its "economic crash"; and the people of Shanghai seem not to be stressed ("yet . . ." he warns) because "the Chinese conceptualise questions about mental states differently from westerners". I see.

Moreover, Britain, Canada and Australia—three "selfish capitalist" nations to which James refers frequently—were not even part of the WHO study of distress. Instead, James uses completely different surveys of national distress for these countries, which he confesses is a "debatable" tactic, because "these studies have not used identical instruments for measuring distress to those employed in the . . . WHO study". On page 31 of this book, he notes: "Comparison can be safely made only between studies in different nations which used the same instruments, in the same way." Yet, ten pages later, he is marrying completely different studies, explaining away the high levels of distress in poor countries like Colombia and the low level of distress in rising capitalist tigers like China.

The book seems packed with caveats about its own scientific claims. James cites [French sociologist] Émile Durkheim's study of suicide in 19th-century Europe, and then writes in parenthesis: "(Durkheim's data has since been queried)." After testing his hypotheses about materialism causing distress, James writes: "The scientifically trained reader will rightly assert that [my] tests of the theory are less than would be needed for a submission to a learned journal." Indeed. Even I, whose scientific training came to an inglorious end with a C grade in GCSE [General Certificate of Secondary Education] physics in 1990, can see that.

Other parts of the book suggest that he might also have a tenuous grip on history. He writes: "Industrialisation and urbanisation are arguably the fundamental causes of high rates of emotional distress." So why didn't people complain about suffering from "low self-esteem", "anxiety" or "impulse disorders" during a historic upheaval such as the British Industrial Revolution? Then, a nation was transformed within a generation: Vast cities were built or expanded and swaths of the population moved from farm work into factories. Life was tough, smelly, unforgiving, yet people somehow survived without the likes of Oliver James or Oprah or Jeremy Kyle [British talk show host] offering them emotional guidance.

No one can possibly believe that people in Britain today have harder emotional lives than those women in shawls who sold soap on misty bridges in Dickensian times, and who had a life expectancy of 46 if they were lucky. Perhaps it is simply that people are more likely to complain about mental hardship these days?

Therapy Culture Is Rampant

James fails fully to interrogate one possible, simple explanation for why Americans, Canadians and Brits allegedly suffer,

> # Economic Growth and Happiness
>
> Economic growth, by itself, certainly isn't enough to guarantee people's well-being. . . . Recent research has also found that some of the things that make people happiest—short commutes, time spent with friends—have little to do with higher incomes.
>
> But it would be a mistake to take this argument too far. The fact remains that economic growth doesn't just make countries richer in superficially materialistic ways.
>
> Economic growth can also pay for investments in scientific research that lead to longer, healthier lives. It can allow trips to see relatives not seen in years or places never visited. When you're richer, you can decide to work less—and spend more time with your friends.
>
> *David Leonhardt,*
> *"Maybe Money Does Buy Happiness After All,"*
> The New York Times, *April 16, 2008.*

or rather claim to suffer, from higher levels of mental distress than others: the "therapy culture". Over the past 30 years, precisely the period in which James says there has been an increase in levels of emotional distress, America has spawned a culture in which we are positively encouraged to discuss everyday problems, from overwork to sadness, as "illnesses" that require therapeutic intervention. In his brilliant *Shyness: How Normal Behavior Became a Sickness*, the American academic Christopher Lane painstakingly shows how the category of "mental disorder" has been expanded in recent decades, so that what were once considered normal emotions or everyday foibles—shyness, rebelliousness, aloofness, and so on—have been relabelled as phobias, disorders and syndromes. The influence of America's therapy culture has been greater in other

English-speaking nations (Britain, Canada, Australia, New Zealand) than it has been in China, for example. It's not that their citizens are more distressed than, say, people struggling to make ends meet in Nigeria (where only 4.7 percent of the population claim to have mental issues), but rather that they are more likely to understand and discuss their problems in these terms.

As you sift through James's claims and data, it is hard to avoid the conclusion that what we have here is plain old prejudice—against garish consumerism, especially of a kind indulged in by the nouveaux riches—dressed up as a scientific study. At heart, this book is deeply conservative: It rehashes the age-old warning that riches will make you unhappy, so you're better off living a simple, smiley life. Because they see overconsumption as the greatest evil, herbal-tea socialists such as James end up not offering solidarity to workers, but constantly warning them that their "greed" will come back to haunt them in the form of a mental disorder. They have rehabilitated the sin of gluttony in pseudo-scientific terms.

I say we should resist the attempts by James and others to relieve us of our "emotional distress". Prickly emotions are frequently the triggers for change, making people strive for better and more meaningful ways of living. James, who advises the government on social policy, argues that "well-being should be a high governmental priority". No, it should not; government-imposed "happiness" or "satisfaction" would only churn out an emotionally complacent populace trained to be satisfied by the simple life. We may all be on the edge—but some of us are looking over it, to see what will come next.

| *"Today, it is much more difficult to con-jure up a consistent picture of luxury living."*

The Consumption of Luxury Goods Is Changing Among Consumers

Knowledge@Wharton

In the following viewpoint, Knowledge@Wharton maintains that the consumption of luxury goods is changing. For instance, it states that buyers of upscale brands are getting younger and luxury has different meanings to today's consumers, so businesses should respond to these customers' unique demands. The publication also claims that high-end names are going mass market through licensing and introducing lower-priced lines, but must protect their image of exclusivity. Knowledge@Wharton is the online business publication of the Wharton School at the University of Pennsylvania.

As you read, consider the following questions:

1. According to the viewpoint, how are younger consumers able to afford luxury brands?

Knowledge@Wharton, "The Luxury Market: Trying to Hit a Moving Target," March 30, 2005. Reproduced by permission.

2. Why does the author claim that the middle market is shrinking?

3. According to the viewpoint, what is a key characteristic of luxury brands?

As the notion of luxury changes, marketers of high-end products are wrestling with the challenge of maintaining brand exclusivity while reaping higher sales, according to executives who spoke on a panel titled, "The New Luxury: Balancing Volume vs. Elite" during Wharton's [the University of Pennsylvania's School of Business] Marketing Conference.

The definition of luxury lifestyle used to translate to an image of old-money Palm Beach, said George Ayres, vice president of marketing for Jaguar North America. Today, it is much more difficult to conjure up a consistent picture of luxury living. People may live in expensive homes and drive luxury cars, but purchase Evian water by the case at Costco and live with barely any furniture, he said. "They might have two bean bag chairs, but they have the car. That's how they decided to express themselves. Other people might drive a Honda Excel, but have a plasma TV."

Many of today's luxury shoppers are not about to wait for the good life, he added. "Guess what? Twenty-five-year-olds have money," Ayres said, adding that the funds for this youthful luxury spending often come from aging, affluent baby boom parents who help finance their children's lifestyle, often out of guilt.

These new definitions of luxury and affluence are making it increasingly difficult to target advertising in the high-end market, according to Ayres. "It's not about demographics anymore," he said, adding that he was once able to focus his advertising in *Architectural Digest*, but now he has to maintain a presence in smaller shelter magazines too, such as *Dwell* and *Wallpaper*. "Now you have to be in all these little places because that's what the 25-year-olds are reading."

A Shopping Experience

According to Edgar Huber, president of the luxury products division at L'Oréal USA, luxury goods manufacturers must constantly balance sales volume against the risk of diminishing the prestige of their brands. Another challenge is consumers' desire to have increasingly personalized products. Distribution channels are also a consideration for luxury-brand marketers, he said. "In cosmetics we are defined not only by innovation and the quality of our products, but it is also very much a shopping experience."

Department stores have dominated cosmetic sales for years, Huber noted, but with the recent turmoil among department store retailers, cosmetics firms are concerned about the strength of their distribution networks. "We have to sell our products and provide this experience in the future. Finding alternate and new ways of selling products will be a key challenge."

Lauren Schickler, vice president of international sales and worldwide marketing at The Movado Group, the 120-year-old Swiss watchmaker, suggested that luxury-brand growth increasingly is tied to licensing. "The new growth platform is all about licensing brands from big multibillion companies and launching products." The goal is not to build brands, but to build categories, said Schickler, who oversees her company's marketing of its Tommy Hilfiger licensed watches.

She pointed out that Hummer has a fragrance, Burberry licenses leather goods, and "Coach is now a lifestyle brand. They have licensed everything from home furnishings to watches to shoes. It's not just a handbag company. Companies are no longer limited by the abilities of their companies to create a luxury category."

She, too, said luxury brand names no longer fit the Palm Beach image. "J. Lo [Jennifer Lopez] is a luxury brand . . . a very aspirational brand, a lifestyle brand." The J. Lo brand is on watches, handbags and jewelry, she noted, adding that

Donald Trump has a fragrance deal with Estée Lauder. "This is what many people are aspiring to be a part of."

Meanwhile, shifting income and demographics have placed tremendous spending power in the hands of young people, including high school girls toting Christian Dior handbags. "The number of young people who have the financial ability to buy luxury goods is astounding," she said. "The demographic is changing significantly. It's now up to us to not only talk to the target, but to understand how the target is shifting, while not alienating the core customer."

Another challenge for luxury names, Schickler added, is managing the growing disparity between the image of the parent brand and licensed products. "The woman or man wearing Gucci is not the same consumer wearing a Gucci watch," she said. Licensing allows an esteemed luxury brand a chance to enter the fashion business. "We don't think about Tommy Hilfiger as watches. They are not timepieces. For us, it's about a fashion statement and being on trend and having a bit of the Tommy Hilfiger franchise on our wrist. It's not about satisfying a consumer need. It's about what you need on your wrist to be relevant to the next season's fashion trends."

Trading Up

Meanwhile, counterfeit and knockoff products remain troublesome for luxury businesses, panelists agreed. "We are fighting as aggressively as we can," said Huber. "It is a very serious issue." Knockoffs do not carry "anywhere near the same emotional benefit" as the genuine article, added Mary Egan, a manager at the Boston Consulting Group who specializes in retail and consumer goods. "I can't say that it's not a problem; it is. But people want the real thing."

According to Egan, high-end manufacturers are struggling to strike a balance between exclusivity and driving volume sales in this period of shifting definitions of what a luxury lifestyle means. "I think the industry is in the process of redefin-

The Emotional Aspects of Brands

While the brand doesn't define luxury, it is the number one most powerful influencer on the luxury consumer when they buy. The second most important influence on luxury consumers is the brand of the store where the luxury product is sold. That means, our luxury brands, including building a brand, communicating its values and using the brand as a conduit to connect to the consumer, is destined to grow as the pivotal axis on which all luxury marketing is based.

What is a brand? Literally it is the "contract" between the company and/or the store and the consumer with the terms written in emotions. It's on an emotional level that consumers connect to brands. Their passion, their loyalty, their dreams and desires are all tied up with the brand.

The stores where we sell our goods and the brands that the stores select to carry are intimately connected in the consumers' mind.

Pam Danziger, "Meet the Butterfly Consumers:
The Evolving New Affluent Consumer," 2003.
www.whypeoplebuy.com.

ing itself. I would say Starbucks is a luxury brand; it's not the same as every luxury brand, but it's an example of a new luxury brand."

Marketers should strive to find ways to dominate the "emotional space" in their category. "Luxury has become so many things," Egan explained. "So many consumers are making decisions on where they want to trade up or trade down. Few can afford to trade up everywhere. How do you find the people who are trading up in your category and are willing to pay the price?" Holding firm to the high-ground of exclusivity may not be an option, she said. "If a luxury brand is purist and doesn't go for mass commercialization, it risks someone else taking the brand and doing the same."

Meanwhile, Egan said the middle market is eroding. "In the old days rich people lived one way." Now, people of all ages and income levels have various aspirations at different stages of life. "If you are in the middle market it's very unstable. You are at risk." To draw the middle market up into luxury price brands, marketers need to make sure their products are credible, Egan suggested. Even if unsophisticated buyers cannot tell the difference between the high-end products and a lower quality substitute, they will take their cue from knowledgeable shoppers who can tell the difference. "If it's not credible to an expert, it's not aspirational to the novice."

Even if a brand reaches out to a broader market, managers must still protect the essence of their luxury product, said Egan. "It's really about how you maintain the image and how you create accessible price points so that people can get a piece of what you are offering, but not the whole thing."

Ayres was asked about Ford's strategy in introducing new lower-priced models selling for $30,000 and whether that would diminish the luster of the Jaguar brand. "Everyone thought we were trying to get 22-year-olds to buy this car, and that is not at all who we are trying to attract," he said. While the entry-level priced Jaguars are designed to sell for $30,000, drivers think it is a $50,000 car, because it is styled like a Jaguar and carries the name, explained Ayres. "They don't have $200,000 a year in income. They have $120,000 in income. A 50-year-old schoolteacher who always wanted her Jaguar—60% of buyers of that car are women. Their income is capped; they are never going to make more. Our challenge is how to capture her, and get her to move up and spend more disposable income on a car."

Egan concluded by saying that despite the challenges and unsettled current state of luxury retailing, the "future of luxury is very bright." She noted that more markets are opening up, and developing countries like Russia, China and India represent huge new markets.

Even in developed nations, she said, there will always be opportunity because people never stop wanting to learn new things. A key characteristic of luxury brands is that they serve to educate people. "People like to learn—from going on a luxury vacation or learning about coffee or looking at car magazines. I think that bodes well for future growth."

> "*False luxury in the age of mass con-*
> *sumption . . . has become so widespread*
> *that true luxury needs to be redefined.*"

Luxury Is Not the Same as Consumer Excess

Joseph Epstein

In the following viewpoint, Joseph Epstein contends that luxury has lost its meaning with the rise of consumerism. In seeking larger markets, high-end brands have lost their cachet and diluted the concept of luxury, Epstein says. What are denoted as luxuries today (e.g., designer labels, "world-class" restaurants) are merely, he insists, hard to obtain, expensive, or ostentatious. Instead, Epstein upholds that real luxury is simpler, quieter, and exists in the beautifully crafted and handsomely rendered. Epstein was editor of The American Scholar *for over twenty years and is the author of numerous books including* Snobbery: The American Version.

As you read, consider the following questions:

1. In Epstein's view, what has happened to the star rating system?

Joseph Epstein, "The Lapse of Luxury: True Splendor Has Many Pretenders, Which Is Why It's in Scant Supply," *Town & Country*, vol. 162, January 2008, p. 116(2). Copyright © 2008 Hearst Communications, Inc. All rights reserved. Reproduced by permission.

2. What "upscale" items, according to Epstein, are costly, but not luxuries?

3. What does the author consider true luxuries?

My late mother, a smart and kindhearted woman, was an unembarrassed materialist. She liked good things, and plenty of them. Her possessions included jewelry, furs, cars and clothes. She had little geographical curiosity, but the one time she traveled to Europe, she flew to Paris on the Concorde and recrossed the Atlantic aboard the *QE2* [*Queen Elizabeth 2*]. Born to immigrant parents, she grew up poor and went on to marry a man raised under essentially the same conditions, who turned out to be a successful moneymaker. She enjoyed the posh and the plush, and he enjoyed giving them to her.

My mother was not easily conned. I recall being in her car, a current-year Cadillac, in crowded traffic at O'Hare Airport in Chicago. I suggested she put her arm out, in hopes that someone would give her a break, allowing her to ease into the flow of traffic. She looked at me as if I were an even greater naif than she had suspected and said: "My dear boy, not likely. When I'm driving this car, others feel that I have already *had* my break."

I'm glad that my mother, who died at eighty-two, did not survive into the age of democratic designer culture. The only designer name I ever heard pass her lips was that of Salvatore Ferragamo, whose shoes she was partial to because they fit her narrow feet well. But I cannot envision my mother worrying about labels. The idea of her walking around with designer logos on her purses, shoes, luggage and silk blouses is un-thinkable. "Just because I buy their clothes," I can hear her say, "I don't see why I also have to walk around advertising them."

My mother was not blind to status, but quality—not sta-tus—was the reason she preferred some things over others. Quality was quality, crappy was crappy, and, sorry, Charlie, but yes, sometimes price was an object, especially if the charge

was for hollow prestige. I cannot imagine her spending $12,000 on a purse, even if it was made of the foreskins of Amazonian alligators and handstitched by Inuit teenagers.

Nor would my mother have fallen for the empty language with which so-called luxury items are now described. Begin with the word *luxury* itself, along with its cousins, *luxe* and *deluxe*. These words have been under quiet but relentless attack through linguistic inflation for decades. The word *luxury*, now everywhere, needs to be examined with a raised eyebrow. Only *luxuriant* retains some value and this as an adjective.

The Inflation of Praise

Words with the suffix *-class* appended to them, once called in to delineate luxury, have long ago lost their ability to describe luxury with anything like precision. The term *first-class*, for example, has been so debased as to be quite without meaning. Granted, first-class air travel is certainly more comfortable than coach, but first-class passengers, let us also grant, far from being genteel society types, are preponderantly salespeople who have racked up lots of free miles. "They said you was high-class," Elvis sang, "but that was just a lie." The old boy was on to something.

World-class is no better, perhaps even a touch worse. World-class hotels, world-class food, world-class singers and symphony orchestras—with such frequency is the word used that it has been drained of any genuine meaning and now even suggests a certain commonplaceness. "Oh, let's not go there," one can imagine a serious snob remarking about a restaurant. "The food and service, I fear, are world-class."

The star system, signifying high luxury, is no longer to be trusted either. So many lackluster restaurants and hotels these days get unearned stars that one wonders if they haven't been self-awarded. I have just returned from lunch at a Chicago steak house that, according to opinions posted online by restaurant-goers, is a five-star eatery. The food was okay, but I'd hold the stars. Movie reviewers also dole out stars, and the most famous among them provide the thumbs-up. (Rarely down, it seems.) Perhaps, given the inflation of praise in our day, before long we shall see films getting two thumbs and an index finger up.

All this inflation of language to denote luxury is owing in part to the rise of consumerism. At the heart of the problem is that when genuinely luxurious goods and institutions have sought larger markets, the people doing the marketing have pumped up the hype used to describe these luxurious things, so that they are now no longer easily separated from merely expensive things and have lost their cachet. Someone trying to move product doesn't figure to be overly scrupulous about the words he uses.

What Is Luxury?

What, then, is luxury in our day? The standard definitions hold it to be something that provides great comfort or extravagant living; sometimes it is defined as an inessential item that is expensive or difficult to obtain. Well, yes and no. As for items difficult to obtain or acquire, rarity isn't necessarily luxury. Rarity is the eyetooth of a cobra, an original Honus Wagner baseball card, an honest used-car salesman. Rarity is out-of-the-way, greatly unusual, all but impossible to get. But it isn't luxury.

Expensive isn't truly luxurious either. When people talk about things being "upscale" or "upmarket," they are really talking about money. And just because something is expensive doesn't mean it's good, let alone luxurious. I have known $350 pens to leak, $70,000 cars to have electrical problems, costly wines to pucker the lips with the taste of tannin. *The New York Times* recently featured a cashmere-lined crocodile bomber jacket for men that costs $52,215; this is not luxury but imbecility.

The last time I stayed at a five-star hotel, it offered the services of a bath butler. This is a man or a woman who draws your bath with certain aromatics in the water and who will add rose petals if you like and arrange for tea or even champagne to accompany your soaking. This doesn't sound like luxury to me but merely harmless decadence.

False luxury in the age of mass consumption, a phrase that captures this affluent time, has become so widespread that true luxury needs to be redefined. While many things are better made than they once were—television sets, automobiles, appliances of all sorts—the small number of things beautifully crafted, or services quietly and handsomely rendered, seems to have diminished.

Luxury is nothing so vulgar as a stretch limo or lighting a cigar with a $100 bill, which are only exhibitions of opulence. Luxury isn't the endless bouts of cosmetic surgery or the $400 male haircut, which are merely costly acts of vanity. Luxury is simpler, sounder. Luxury is the small hotel with unobtrusive yet perfect service, with no cloying chocolates left on one's pillow. Luxury is the elegant dinner, served without talk of presentation or herbs, in which the only things that come through are the fine flavors of the food and wine and the care that has gone into the meal's preparation. Luxury is the coat or dress or suit that has been made with the kind of attention to the details of cloth and color and cut and stitching that to wear it magically lifts the spirits.

My mother would have recognized such luxury by instinct, and so, my strong hunch is, do you.

Periodical Bibliography

The following articles have been selected to supplement the diverse views presented in this chapter.

George Blecher   "Conspicuous Consumption, a Century On," *spiked*, May 26, 2004.

Lesley Blume   "Luxury as an Investment?" *The Big Money*, May 6, 2009.

Judith H. Dobrzynski "The End of Conspicuous Philanthropy?" *Forbes*, May 5, 2009.

Al Donohue   "Increasing Wealth Drives Luxury Market," *The Ridgewood News*, July 13, 2007.

Oliver James   "Earn More, Want More, Spend More," *Telegraph*, May 4, 2007.

Steve Kendall   "How Looking Poor Became the New Status Symbol," *Details*, June/July 2009.

Marketing   "Ethics of Marketing: It's More than Enough to Make You Sick," January 23, 2009.

Marketing Week   "To Buy or Not to Buy," November 22, 2007.

Kimberly Palmer   "Pollster Predicts a More Spiritual Shift," *U.S. News & World Report*, August 26, 2008.

CHAPTER 2

What Facilitates
Consumerism?

Chapter Preface

On September 27, 2001, president George W. Bush held a rally for airline safety at Chicago O'Hare International Airport, less than three weeks after the terrorist attacks on the World Trade Center and the Pentagon. Bush urged citizens to "fly and enjoy America's great destination spots. Go down to Disney World in Florida, take your families, and enjoy life the way we want it to be enjoyed."[i] Some pundits construed him as imploring the nation to spend to fight terrorism. Political blogger Steve Clemons said, "Bush told Americans that the best way that they can help America during its time of crisis was to keep shopping, flying planes, and going to the malls."[ii]

While Bush's remarks are open to interpretation, American culture is punctuated with mottos that signalize consumerism as a national pastime, such as "Shop 'til you drop!" and "When the going gets tough, the tough go shopping!" In fact, John F. Schumaker, an American psychologist living in New Zealand, left the United States because its culture allegedly promotes consumerism. "While most societies throughout history have organized themselves in order to curb natural greed," he alleges, "America's devoted consumers are encouraged to respect, nurture, and act on the subtlest stirrings of their avarice. As a result, materialism has reached fever pitch and continues to rise sharply."[iii] Schumaker continues that the "world seems hell-bent on following America's lead. But there is nothing useful to be learned from the American Dream in its present hyper-commercialized form."

Yet, other commentators claim that consumer behavior and trends have distinct societal meanings and do not mimic so-called American consumerism abroad. According to busi-

i. *Washington Post*, September 27, 2001.
ii. *Washington Note*, October 12, 2004.
iii. *New Internationalist*, July 2001.

ness experts Douglas B. Holt, John A. Quelch, and Earl L. Taylor, "The rise of a global culture doesn't mean that consumers share the same tastes or values. Rather, people in different nations, often with conflicting viewpoints, participate in a shared conversation, drawing upon shared symbols."[iv] For example, scholars Jagdish Sheth, Naresh Malhotra, and Eric J. Arnould said, "Thanks to local modifications of the McDonald's formula, the Jolibee fast-food chain at one time enjoyed a 59 percent market share in the Philippine fast-food market."[v]In the following chapter, the authors debate what factors shape consumerism and encourage consumer behavior.

iv. *Harvard Business Review*, September 2004.
v. *Encyclopedia of International Marketing*, 2008.

> *"The sophistication of advertising methods and techniques has advanced, enticing and shaping and even creating consumerism and needs where there has been none before."*

Advertising Promotes Consumerism

Anup Shah

In the following viewpoint, Anup Shah argues that advertising in the media fuels consumerism. He maintains that because of increasing corporate competition, companies spend billions of dollars on advertising to persuade people to buy what they do not need. In fact, audiences of television programs, movies, newspapers, and magazines, according to Shah, have become products that the media sell to advertisers. Furthermore, the author claims that multinational companies are globalizing consumerism by influencing consumption attitudes and habits in cultures across the world through advertising. Shah is the founder of Global Issues, *an international news and commentary Web site based in England.*

Anup Shah, "Media and Advertising," *Global Issues*, January 26, 2008. Copyright © 2008. Reproduced by permission. www.globalissues.org.

As you read, consider the following questions:

1. According to the author, what is an "advertorial"?

2. As stated by Shah, why may magazine articles be "dumbed down"?

3. Why is product placement becoming more pervasive, in Shah's opinion?

Advertising is the art of arresting the human intelligence just long enough to get money from it.

—Chuck Blore,
a partner in the advertising firm Chuck Blore
& Don Ruchman, Inc., quoted by Ben H. Bagdikian,
The Media Monopoly, *Sixth Edition (Beacon Press), p.185.*

Ever since mass media became mass media, companies have naturally used this means of communications to let a large number of people know about their products. There is nothing wrong with that, as it allows innovative ideas and concepts to be shared with others. However, as the years have progressed, the sophistication of advertising methods and techniques has advanced, enticing and shaping and even creating consumerism and needs where there has been none before, or turning luxuries into necessities. This [viewpoint] introduces some of the issues and concerns this raises.

Free Media Channels Have a Cost

Various free media, such as the numerous channels available in America and other nations, are naturally subsidized with advertising to help pay the costs.

As corporate competition has increased, so too has the need for returns on massive expenditures on advertising. Industries spend millions, even billions of dollars to win our hearts and minds, and to influence our choices towards their products and ideas. This often means such media outlets attract greater funds than those outlets funded through public

funding or TV licenses. It can mean that such outlets can also then afford better programming of key events and programs.

The sheer amount of money this brings to media companies is significant and in many cases forms the main form of support for the media company. Hence, if something is reported that the advertiser doesn't like, the media company risks losing much needed revenue to stay alive.

As a result, the mainstream media is largely driven by the forces of the market.

The Audience as the Product

Additionally, as [American philosopher] Noam Chomsky points out in his article, "What Makes Mainstream Media Mainstream," for a company such as The New York Times, it too has to sell products to its customers. For The New York Times and other such companies, Chomsky points out that the product is the audience, and the customers are the corporate advertisers.

This at first thought doesn't seem to make sense. However, although readers buy the paper, he argues that readers fit a demography and it is this that is valuable information that can be used by advertisers. Hence, to the advertisers, the product that The New York Times and such companies bring to them is the audience itself and it is the advertisers that bring the money to the media companies, not the audience.

> [T]he New York Times [is] a corporation and sells a product. The product is audiences. They don't make money when you buy the newspaper. They are happy to put it on the World Wide Web for free. They actually lose money when you buy the newspaper. But the audience is the product. . . . You have to sell a product to a market, and the market is, of course, advertisers (that is, other businesses). Whether it is television or newspapers, or whatever, they are selling audiences. Corporations sell audiences to other corporations.

The Audience Also as the Consumer

Ben Bagdikian, a prominent media critic and author of the well-acclaimed book *The Media Monopoly*, provides more detail and examples. In Chapter 6 of his book, for example, Bagdikian describes in detail the pressure on media companies to change content (to "dumb down") and to shape content based on the demographics of the audiences. Slowly then, the content of media isn't as important as the type of person being targeted by the ads.

He also shows that the notion of "giving the audience what they want" is also a bit misleading because, if anything, it is more about targeting those readers that can afford the products that are advertised and so it is almost like giving the advertisers what they want!

The "dumbing down" of the content also acts to promote a "buying mood." Hence, as Bagdikian summarizes, "programming is carefully noncontroversial, light, and nonpolitical." As he traces briefly the history of advertising in magazines he also hints that this has happened for a long time:

The influence of advertising on magazines reached a point where editors began selecting articles not only on the basis of their expected interest for readers but for their influence on advertisements. Serious articles were not always the best support for ads. An article that put the reader in an analytical frame of mind did not encourage the reader to take seriously an ad that depended on fantasy or promoted a trivial product. An article on genuine social suffering might interrupt the "buying" mood on which most ads for luxuries depend. The next step, seen often in mid-twentieth century magazines, was commissioning articles solely to attract readers who were good prospects to buy products advertised in the magazine. After that came the magazine phenomenon of the 1970s—creating magazines for an identifiable special audience and selling them to particular advertisers.

Advertorials—Advertisements Disguised as News!

Sometimes, news stories or editorials are often subtle product advertisements, even with a rise of new terms in critical circles, such as "advertorials."

In other cases, due to large ownership, a news company will advertise another program belonging to the parent network and highlight it as a news story, as some "reality TV" programs in America, such as the *Survivor* series, have shown. Another example is the hype on ABC News of Disney's *Pearl Harbor* movie (Disney owns ABC), which some have even described as propaganda. Examples abound, and it would be a futile effort to attempt to list them all here. Such use of news time to promote entertainment has come under criticism of late. [Anthropologist] Richard Robbins also captures this well:

Protected by the free speech provision of the First Amendment, corporations marshal huge public relations efforts on behalf of their agendas. In the United States the 170,000 public relations employees whose job it is to manipulate news, public opinion and public policy in the interests of their clients outnumber news reporters by 40,000. A study in 1990 discovered that almost 40 percent of the news content of a typical U.S. newspaper originates as public relations press releases, story memos, and suggestions. The *Columbia Journalism Review* reported that more than half the news stories in *The Wall Street Journal* are based solely on corporate press releases (cited in Korten 1995:146 [When Corporations Rule the World]). United States corporations spend almost half as much on advertising (approximately $120 per person) as the state spends on education ($207 per person).

On April 7, 2002, UK's BBC aired a documentary called *Century of the Self* looking back at the rise of consumerism in the 20th century. In discussing the role of the media, it was pointed out how journalism also changed as big business started to gain more influence. Many, in order to get stories that would attract readers, would have to agree to editorial content being dictated by business, such as placement of specific advertising in the pictures, placing certain sentences and paragraphs, and mentioning key products related to the story, etc.

A number of scandals erupted in 2005 revealed all manner of fake news and media manipulation. . . .

Advertainment—Advertisements Disguised as Entertainment!

We are also seeing more sophisticated techniques, such as short films where the aim is to sell a product but to cleverly do the advertising in a subtle way. These mini films can be very entertaining and exciting, but also promote a product behind the main theme.

While it could be argued that there is nothing wrong with this, it is just a more sophisticated way to sell products, more forthcoming and explicit mention that this is a commercial would be good for more people to be aware of what they are watching. (Although, that might be as hard as asking a government to tell their audience that they are about to watch some propaganda and to take it in appropriate consideration!)

Also, the enormous sums of money that can back up this sort of entertainment versus others can, in the long run, further affect the type and diversity of the content we receive. [According to journalist Erika Milvy:]

> In fact, "brand-sponsored content" as [producer] Steve Golin likes to call this, is as old as television. Today, many gripe that the World Wide Web is nothing but a World Wide Commercial for which securing eyeballs for advertisers is the first and last concern. Lest we forgot, TV was also invented to sell to us in the comfort of our home. Content has always been an afterthought. At the dawn of TV, soap operas got their name from the soap that was hawked by the show's sponsors, who exercised a good deal of control over the shows themselves (which existed merely to fill the space between commercials).

Product Placement

As Milvy has noted above, advertisements in television programming go back to the beginnings of television. These days, whether you are watching a film from Bollywood (India's film industry) or Hollywood, there will be some obvious advertisements and some not-so-obvious ones.

This "product placement" is becoming more pervasive. Also noting the old-age of product placement in films, [Jonathan Duffy of] the BBC also adds that it is now also extending to other forms of entertainment:

> Cinema-goers will be familiar with product placement in films: those countless examples where the camera lingers just a little too long over a logo before shifting back to the main action. Now, more than 50 years after Hollywood wised up to the fact that companies will pay to have their brands featured within the narrative of a movie, advertisers have

begun to extend the principle to formats such as books, pop songs, videos and computer games.

This therefore begs the question (Duffy also asks), "Who is in charge—the producer or the product brand manager?"

Duffy also adds, "Research shows that in programmes recorded, two-thirds to 80% of ads are skipped." That is, people don't want to watch advertising. Hence, the increased interest in placing brands in actual programming where it is sometimes less obvious. . . .

Globalization of Consumers

As globalization becomes ever more prominent, the role of media and advertising and consumerism also increases. Ideal for the large multinationals that can take best advantage of globalization include the even larger "market" to which products can be sold. However, diverse cultures could sometimes be an obstacle to easy selling. Ideally then, attitudes and consumption habits need to be similar for best effect. As a result many media companies promote and project a more aligned culture that will cross these boundaries but also allow easier consumption of their products. The United Nations Development Programme's 1998 Human Development Report summarizes this quite well:

> Globalization is integrating not just trade, investment and financial markets. It is also integrating consumer markets. . . . [Economically,] there is fierce competition to sell to consumers worldwide, with increasingly aggressive advertising.

> On the social side, local and national boundaries are breaking down in the setting of social standards and aspirations in consumption. Market research identifies "global elites" and "global middle classes" who follow the same consumption styles, showing preferences for "global brands". There are the "global teens"—some 270 million 15- to 18-year-olds in 40 countries—inhabiting a "global space", a single pop-

culture world, soaking up the same videos and music and providing a huge market for designer running shoes, T-shirts and jeans.

... At the same time the consumer receives a flood of information through commercial advertising. An average American, it is estimated, sees 150,000 advertisements on television in his or her lifetime. And advertising is increasing worldwide, faster than population or incomes. Global advertising spending, by the most conservative reckoning, is now $435 billion.

Also worth quoting at some length is part of a [2001] paper [by Richard C. Vincent] looking at democracy and transnational media, labeled "promotion of consumerism at all costs":

The leading transnational media giants are often American or at least Western corporations. To expand markets they must continue to look for new regions for expansion. Southeast Asia, for example, may be one of the last major regions to be affected by international satellites.

It really was not until the 1990s, for example, that Southeast Asia saw Western television enter on a massive scale. Advances in technology plus market liberalization were reasons. Asia, of course, is the largest worldwide market (2.8 billion) and has one-third of the world's television sets. While Asia has been known to foster a distinct culture and linguistic heritage, this specialty is now in jeopardy. We see MTV, Western news and movie channels, and other Western media influences spreading across Asia. The cultural heritage of these countries is being threatened by trans border data flow, media images moving across national borders, thanks to new electronic forms of media delivery. People are told they need products they never "realized" they required. They are told via media that Western styles and habits may be better or more desirable than their own traditions and customs. Young people in particular now grow up with stronger ties to New York and Los Angeles than their own capitals and families.

Then there is the danger that comes when making money is more important than quality of information flow. China's 1.2 billion people are a very desirable audience. Consider what happened when News Corporation purchased STAR TV in 1993. A controversial program on the Chinese government on *BBC World Television News* lead to PRC official complaints. [News Corporation chairman Rupert] Murdoch simply pulled the plug. Note that he also was an investor in the *Beijing People's Daily*. Similar pressures caused him to pressure HarperCollins of London to cancel a book contract with a former ambassador to China because it too was critical of the regime.

The problem goes beyond economic concentrations. Because the product of media industries is cultural programming, the concern centers on the very fabric of life.

As stated earlier, the movement is toward grabbing attention and creating a desire for things that people never knew was needed. It also is about using the media to homogenize culture. It involves the world's children, even in the most communication-savvy communities where children below the age of ten are targeted with clever media campaigns. Yet these children are incapable of cognitively understanding what media does. Hence we have animated television programs as those developed several years ago, *He-Man* and *She Ra*, where the programs primarily were introduced to market massive lines of toys for the Christmas season. We are submitting innocent children to strategies of a mega-million dollar advertising industry and most parents are incapable of responding to sales campaigns of this magnitude. MTV is another example. Here we have entertainment programming which doubles as a continuous commercial for music CDs, clothing lines, talk shows involving music personalities, and a variety of other marketing ploys.

> "Consumption without need is the hall-
> mark of addiction, and 'consumerism'
> is defined as 'the equating of personal
> happiness with the purchasing of mate-
> rial possessions and consumption.'"

Shopping Addiction Promotes Consumerism

Charles Shaw

*In the following viewpoint, Charles Shaw contends that the ad-
diction to consumption—out-of-control buying of unnecessary
goods for personal fulfillment—compounds America's problem
with consumerism. In his view, compulsive and addictive shopping develops as a reaction to traumatic events or personal issues, which is exacerbated by an economic system that reinforces
consumerism and marketing tactics that appeal to unconscious
desires and unmet needs. The accompanying moral and ethical
decline, Shaw also upholds, will continue until consumer culture
hits rock bottom. The author is a journalist and activist from
Chicago.*

Charles Shaw, "Viewing Consumer Culture Through the Lens of Addiction," Huffington
Post, June 6, 2008. Reproduced by permission. www.huffingtonpost.com.

As you read, consider the following questions:

1. How does the author characterize people with materialistic values?

2. According to Shaw, how has consumerism been "naturalized"?

3. How is the addiction to consumerism more dangerous than substance abuse, in Shaw's view?

"An addict is someone who uses their body to tell society that something is wrong."

—Stella Adler (1901–1992)

In last year's [2007] powerful independent documentary, *What a Way to Go: Life at the End of Empire*, producer Sally Erickson pulled from her 20 years working as a therapist in private practice to attempt to explain why so many people, perhaps even you, are so unhappy.

The film from writer-director [Timothy S.] Bennett is an epic exploration of a Middle American, middle-class white father of three coming to grips with climate change, resource crises, environmental meltdown and the demise of the American lifestyle. It is as compassionate a film as it is utterly terrifying.

Through a pastiche of revolutionary thinkers including Derrick Jensen, Daniel Quinn, Jerry Mander, Richard Manning and Chellis Glendinning, *What a Way to Go* concludes that industrial civilization—and its end product, consumerism—has disconnected us from nature, the cycle of life, our communities, our families and, ultimately, ourselves. This unnatural, inorganic, materialistic way of living, coupled with a marked decline in society's moral and ethical standards—what the French call anomie—has created a kind of pathology that produces pain and emptiness, for which addictive behavior becomes the primary symptom and consumption the preferred drug of choice.

"What most of us experience when it comes to addiction," says Erickson, "is a pattern of continually seeking more of what it is we don't really want and, therefore, never being fully satisfied. And as long as we are never satisfied, we continue to seek more, while our real needs are never being met."

"Addiction in one form or another characterizes every aspect of industrial society," wrote the social philosopher Morris Berman, and dependence on substances or corporeal pleasures is no different from dependence on "prestige, career achievement, world influence, wealth, the need to build more ingenious bombs or the need to exercise control over everything."

At the very least, this certainly raises questions about the dominant, socially accepted view of addiction, the disempowering, less-than-hospitable "disease model," which claims addiction is a chronic illness predetermined by genetics. The "disease model" is characterized by a loss of control over substances or practices, along with denial of the severity and consequences of using or engaging in them.

"Current research shows that genetics are the most significant factor in addiction," argues Bruce Sewick, a Chicago area substance abuse clinician who works with the mentally ill. "A person is four times more likely to become dependent on alcohol or drugs when there is a genetic history of the same."

The Hallmark of Our Era

This may be true, but the pervasive pattern of addictive behavior that finds its way into our economics, our politics, and our interpersonal relationships cannot be just explained away using genetic predeterminism. Consumption without need is the hallmark of addiction, and "consumerism" is defined as "the equating of personal happiness with the purchasing of material possessions and consumption." The pattern of out-of-control consumption in the United States, which per capita consumes 70 times more than India, with three times the U.S. population, is not qualitatively different from the well-known patterns of behavior of substance abusers. In fact, it looks as if the United States just finished with the worst binge of its life and is now cresting the peak of a wicked crash.

"I think consumerism is probably a bit of an addiction," offers Richard Eckersley, an Australian public health researcher featured in a 2003 radio documentary, *Consumerism, Money, and Happiness*:

> Addiction is really a hallmark of our era, and I think it reflects that we don't have culturally promoted kinds of other deeper forms of meaning and purpose in our lives. So we make up for it by consuming more. But the evidence is overwhelming that people who are characterized by materialistic attitudes and values actually experience lower well-being, lower happiness, more depression and anxiety and anger than people who aren't materialistic.

While we generally accept that anything can be used addictively, we often tend to forget or overlook why it's being used in the first place. Most professionals will agree that the purpose or function of an addiction is to put a buffer between ourselves and the experience or awareness of our emotions. An addiction serves to numb us so that we are out of touch with what we know and what we feel. Eventually this numb buffer zone becomes a habituated coping mechanism.

"But addiction itself," explains Tom Goforth, a Christian minister and practicing clinical psychotherapist for more than 40 years, "is not innate to the human species. It's something we developed to cope with our predicament."

Over the years Goforth saw most of the addictions he treated develop as the result of some violation of the self, a deep wounding or trauma. This wounding can come from any number of causes: domestic violence and abuse, prejudice and racism, warfare, economic hardship, illness and death, even something as insidiously mundane as rejection, shame, insecurity or feelings of inadequacy.

Primitivist writer-activists like Derrick Jensen and Chellis Glendinning believe that consumer culture drives the "culture of empire," an inherently abusive system built on resource exploitation and the subjugation of peoples. Because of this, those living in it have undergone a collective wounding or trauma that has left society suffering from a mass form of PTSD [post-traumatic stress disorder].

Glendinning is the author of *My Name Is Chellis and I'm in Recovery from Western Civilization*, a book that examines the relationship between addiction and the ecological crisis. In an essay on what she calls "techno-addiction" Glendinning writes about our "primary" and "secondary" sources of satisfaction. "Primary" needs are those we were born to have satisfied: nourishment, love, meaning, purpose and spirit. When they are not met, we turn to the "secondary" sources, which include "drugs, violence, sex, material possessions and machines." Eventually we become obsessed with the secondary sources "as if our lives depended on them."

Naturalizing Addictions

Designing and marketing secondary sources of satisfaction falls to the complimenting social, political and economic systems that reinforce addictive behavior in order to drive the consumer machine. Consumption becomes "naturalized" through corporate advertising and marketing, government tax breaks, and officially sanctioned religio-consumer holidays like Christmas, Hanukah and Valentine's Day. Let us never forget that after 9/11 [President] George Bush told Americans it was their patriotic duty to "spend."

"Everything appalling has to be naturalized in order to be justified," says Derrick Jensen, author of the Endgame series and *The Culture of Make Believe*. "This is because an abusive system is designed to protect the abuser. The whole idea of naturalizing addictions is about maintaining the dependency and victimhood of the addict, the abused."

In a system based on consumption, the best patient a doctor, therapist or pharmacist can ask for is one who never gets better. Is it any coincidence then that in the dominant model an addict always remains an addict? Under this rubric, the addict is always "recovering" and never "recovered." Imagine the psychological impact of imposing a perpetual sense of powerlessness on someone. It must be profound. But it suddenly makes a whole lot more sense when you look at the few socially acceptable surrogates like AA, Prozac, work or Jesus. Aren't these, in a sense, meant to be chronic as well? This approach simply transfers the dependency while preserving the overall system of consumptive behavior.

By the same token, what better consumer can a corporation ask for than one who is never satisfied with what they buy, who always has to have the next, the biggest, the newest in order to feel like they are somebody. If real needs were being met, it's a good possibility that certain markets would contract or collapse. Knowing this, our identities have in a sense been re-engineered to accommodate forced obsolescence, so that every few years we're told we need an upgrade. Tellingly, we call it our "new look" or the "new you." Whole industries are based in this.

Naturalizing addictions through consumerism has its beginnings in early 20th century notions of psychology and social control. The story of how consumerism, and more importantly, the consumer self, came into being is the subject of Adam Curtis's BBC documentary *The Century of the Self*. It is, at its core, the story of Sigmund Freud.

In response to the barbarism of Nazi Germany during the Second World War, which Freud believed was unleashed by the dangerous and irrational fears and desires that lay deep within the unconscious, Western politicians and planners set about finding ways to control this "hidden enemy within the human mind."

One of the theories that emerged was the brainchild of Freud's nephew, Edward Bernays, the sloganeering progenitor of public relations who helped Woodrow Wilson sell the First World War to the American public by inventing the tag line, "Making the World Safe for Democracy." "[PR] is really just propaganda," Bernays says in the film, "but we couldn't use the word because the Germans had."

Bernays showed American corporations how to make people buy material goods they didn't need by connecting those products to their unconscious desires and unmet needs. This made him incredibly powerful and in demand. He used this influence to propose that the same principles be used politically to control the masses.

This social-control-through-indulgence model was later excoriated in Aldous Huxley's *Brave New World*, a critique of consumerism and the vapidity of a culture based in pleasure seeking. In Huxley's futuristic dystopia, freethinking and human attachment have either been outlawed or genetically modified out of most of humanity. In its place is a dumbed-down hierarchical society overrun by high-tech entertainment, sexual promiscuity and a powerful, all-purpose intoxicant/narcotic/dissociative drug called Soma, which is used to quell any unpleasant feelings. Perhaps this sounds familiar?

Time for Intervention

"We can see where consumer psychology has led us," Tom Goforth sighs heavily. "It's a disaster. It's the kind of thing that has caused the human organism and psyche to go so far out of balance. Marketing to our unconscious leads us down a dangerous path that promises satisfaction and wholeness and a sense of importance and worth without us having to do anything but spend. But none of these things come in any real sense unless we work hard at them."

The ego, Freud discovered, is the part of us that invests in the values of society that hold out fulfillment for us. We as in-

Unhappiness and Impulse Shopping

Like drinking too much or eating too much, the root cause of impulse shopping is unhappiness, says Coquitlam, B.C., psychologist Denis Boyd. Impulse shoppers buy because they crave an emotional lift. Pronto. Wobbly marriages can spawn it, Boyd explains, and high-pressure jobs feed it. "It's a cousin to shoplifting," he says, "where people steal when they don't need to." Impulse shoppers have reported collecting thousands of wrenches, for example. But Boyd, who treats compulsive shoppers of both sexes, thinks men and women seek different thrills. "Women see their personalities reflected in their homes," he says, so they load up on candle holders and Cuisinarts, or they travel, or do both.

Barbara Righton,
"Hooked on the Spending High: Compulsive Shopping
Is Pushing Millions to the Brink of Financial Ruin,"
Maclean's, *November 26, 2007.*

dividual human beings may be looking for fulfillment through our contribution to society and our own sense of meaning, integrity, love and connection. "But instead," Goforth says, "consumerism teaches the ego to let go of integrity and inflate itself with an aesthetic, material process that confuses, or associates, self-worth with net worth."

This is the gospel preached by activist-performance-artist Reverend Billy of the Church of Stop Shopping, star of the upcoming *What Would Jesus Buy?*, an anti-consumer road film produced by *Super Size Me's* Morgan Spurlock. Rev. Billy preaches that consumerism has become our great national addiction.

"If we're ever going to move away from being consumers and back to being citizens, society will need to go into recovery," says the good reverend. "I recommend at least 60 to 90 days away from the shopping just to detox if we don't repent," he warns, "then the Shopocalypse is coming!"

Asking society to go into a global recovery program is not nearly as [self-help expert] Dr. Phil–crazy as it sounds. It's become the new mantra of the green movement, who are now calling for a spiritual solution to the planetary crisis. It was Freud's student and eventual rival Carl Jung who first dissented against Freud's "irrational desires" theory and put forth the idea that addictions address a spiritual loss or deficiency. Because the addictive experience is mimetic of the spiritual experience, you can have an imitation of bliss or oneness, but it doesn't last. Jung believed only a true spiritual awakening will end an addiction. Likewise, the eco-ilk believe only a global spiritual awakening will end the consumer addiction that is ravaging the planet.

In *Steps to an Ecology of Mind*, Gregory Bateson, the evolutionary philosopher husband of anthropologist Margaret Mead, observed that addictive behavior is consistent with the Western approach to life that pits mind against body. Because of this schism, Bateson gave our species a low probability of continued survival.

"In order to avoid this literal death," Derrick Jensen adds soberly, "society will have to go through a cultural death and spiritual rebirth."

Heady words for sure, but it may be our only way out of this mess. For this process to begin, consumer society must first "hit bottom." Let us hope this happens soon. As Sally Erickson reminds us, the patterns of behavior endemic to consumer society are so much more dangerous than substance abuse, because they are perpetuating a culture that is literally eating itself out of house and home. If addicts define insanity as doing the same thing over and over again, and expecting different results, this may be the clearest sign yet that consumerism is driving us all crazy.

But there is hope to leave you with. In his 40 years treating addicts, Tom Goforth will honestly tell you that, by and large, those who did truly conquer their addictions became less materialistic and more aligned with a sense of who they really were and what they felt their life purpose was.

Maybe it's time for that intervention.

| *"Consumerism was a necessary compo-
nent of US capitalism from the 1820s
to the 1970s."*

Capitalism
Promotes Consumerism

Rick Wolff

*In the following viewpoint, Rick Wolff states that the economics
of capitalism spread consumerism—now uncontrolled, ecologically harmful, and fiscally disastrous—throughout the United
States. According to Wolff, capitalists paid workers' rising real
wages from 1820 to 1970, encouraging them to consume more—
and work harder—each decade. He adds that dominant social
groups also reinforced consumption as the goal of work and the
measure of personal worth. When real wages stopped rising,
Wolff insists that deeply rooted consumerist values continued to
push Americans to work harder and borrow more to buy
more—to the point of emotional and financial collapse. Wolff is
a professor of economics at the University of Massachusetts at
Amherst and co-author of* Class Theory and History: Capitalism and Communism in the U.S.S.R *and* New Departures in
Marxian Theory.

Rick Wolff, "Consumerism: Curses and Causes," *Monthly Review*, April 30, 2008. Copyright © 2008 by MR Press. Reproduced by permission of Monthly Review Foundation.
www.monthlyreview.org.

As you read, consider the following questions:

1. How does Wolff define consumerism?

2. How did the income gap between workers and employers widen, in the author's opinion?

3. According to Wolff, how did consumerism lead to the subprime mortgage crisis of 2008?

US consumerism—citizens driven excessively to buy goods and services and accumulate consumable wealth—is cursed almost everywhere. Many environmentalists blame it for global warming. Critics of the current economic disasters often point to home-buying gluttony as the cause. Many see consumerism behind the borrowing that makes the US the world's greatest debtor nation today. Moralists of otherwise diverse motivations agree on attacking consumerist materialism as against spiritual values. Educators blame it for distracting young people's interest from learning. Psychologists attribute mass loneliness and depression to unrealizable expectations of what commodities can deliver to consumers. Physicians decry the diseases, stress, and exhaustion linked to excessive work driven by desire for excessive consumption. Yet, for a long time, exhortations by all such folks have mostly failed to slow, let alone reverse, US consumerism.

The question is why? The answer is not advertising, since that begs the question of why that industry should have been so successful in the US and grown to such influence. Nor is it plausible to attribute some national personality flaw to our citizens.

The Unique History of US Capitalism

A big part of the answer lies in the unique history of US capitalism. From 1820 to 1970, over every decade, average real wages rose enabling a rising standard of consumption. These 150 years rooted workers' beliefs that the USA was a "chosen" place where every generation would live better than its parents. This was "the good news" of US capitalism for the workers. The "bad news" was that the average worker's productivity—the amount of output each worker produced for his/her employer to sell—rose even faster. This was because workers were relentlessly driven by employers to work harder, faster, and with ever more (and more complicated) machinery. Thus, alongside rising workers' wages, faster rising productivity brought even bigger gains for employers.

An unspoken, historic deal defined US capitalism for those 150 years. Capitalists paid rising wages to enable rising working class consumption; the workers had to provide rising work effort, rising profitability, and thus the even faster rise of profits. *Because the rise in workers' consumption was slower than the rise of their productivity—the output that they delivered to employers—the gap between workers and employers widened across US history.* A fundamentally unequal society emerged, one that forever mocked, challenged, and undermined the ideological claims of the US to be the land of equality and opportunity. The working class labored ever harder, consumed more, and yet fell ever further behind the minority who lived off the growing difference between what workers produced and their wages.

This deal might have collapsed at any time if US workers rebelled against the organization of production in the US. This could have occurred if rising wages did not suffice to make them ignore the growing inequality of US life, or if they rejected subordination to ever more automated, exhausting work disciplines, or if they refused to deliver ever more wealth to ever fewer corporate boards of directors of immense corporations ever further removed from them in power, wealth, and access to culture. For that deal to survive—for US capitalism to have been "successful" for so long—something had to emerge in US society that prevented any of these deal-breakers from happening. Enter consumerism!

The idea settled into US culture that consumption was the proper goal of work and the measure of personal worth, of one's "success" in life. Business boosters and ideologues pushed that idea, but they were hardly alone. Advertisers made it their constant message. Trade unions focused also on raising wages and consumption—just what US capitalism could and did deliver—rather than challenging the organization of production. So too did most left movements. Economists did their part by building modern economics on the unquestioned axiom that labor was a burden for which consumption enabled by wages was the compensation. This definition of economics required banishing the alternative of Marxian economics [after the theories of Karl Marx, who opposed capitalism] from schools. The mass media proceeded as if it were likewise obvious common sense that all any employee *really* cared about was the size of his/her wage/salary. Of course, some dissident voices—especially on the left—rejected these ideas and this capital/labor deal, but consumerism usually all but drowned them out.

The Deal Has Been Broken

Consumerism's deep roots in the psyche of US workers explains their reactions when real wages stopped rising in the 1970s and since. They simply kept on buying more commodities. To pay for them, workers took on more hours of labor and borrowed vast sums. Worker exhaustion rose accordingly, likewise the number of family members sent out to work (straining "family values" to the breaking point). Anxiety intensified over frightening family debt levels. In this situation, the current scandal of sub-prime mortgages [a type of loan granted to individuals with poor credit histories, with a higher interest rate because of the increased risk to lenders] was a predictable disaster waiting to happen.

The 150-year deal has been broken. The business side no longer needs it; it hasn't since the 1970s. That is why real

Consumers Call the Tune

What is called "capitalism" might more accurately be called consumerism. It is the consumers who call the tune, and those capitalists who want to remain capitalists have to learn to dance to it. The twentieth century began with high hopes for replacing the competition of the marketplace by a more efficient and more humane economy, planned and controlled by government in the interests of the people. However, by the end of the century, all such efforts were thoroughly discredited by their actual results in the countries around the world that even communist nations abandoned central planning, while socialist governments in democratic countries began selling off government-run enterprises, whose chronic losses had been a heavy burden to the taxpayers.

Privatization was embraced as a principle by such conservative governments as those of Prime Minister Margaret Thatcher in Britain and President Ronald Reagan in the United States. But the most decisive evidence for the efficiency of the marketplace was that even socialist and government leaders who were philosophically opposed to capitalism turned back towards the free market after seeing what happens when industry and commerce operate without guidance of prices, policies, profits and losses.

Thomas Sowell,
"Part II: Industry and Commerce: 8: An Overview,"
Basic Economics: A Common Sense Guide to the Economy.
3rd ed. Cambridge, MA: Basic Books, 2007, p. 178.

wages stopped rising. Most workers just postponed facing that reality and its implications: by having more family members do more work and by heavy borrowing. Meanwhile, able and willing laborers abroad who accept wages far lower than in the US beckon. US corporations are moving to produce there. They will ship "home" the goods and services they produce abroad so long as US citizens can afford them. When that no longer pays, they will redirect shipments to the rest of the world market.

Consumerism was a necessary component of US capitalism from the 1820s to the 1970s. As an ideology uniquely suited to that capitalism, it was articulated, cultivated, and supported by different social groups. Whatever fun comedians and critics poke at consumerism, it was not some lovable human foible, nor some quirk of our culture. It was the glue holding US capitalism together for a long time. Even more important, business dissolved that glue in the 1970s, and now US workers have exhausted ways to postpone the results of that dissolution. Storms are rising.

| "We are showing that consumerism is a choice, not something we are coerced into doing."

Capitalism Is Confused with Consumerism

Michael J. Foster

In the following viewpoint, Michael J. Foster shows that consumerism and capitalism are not necessarily the same thing. Foster uses his personal experience as a freegan to show that consumerism is a choice. A capitalist supporter can still make choices as a consumer by looking at the cost of the consumption, the negative externalities, and the other choices, Foster explains. Foster is a biodiversity specialist, environmental policy analyst, and a contributor to Earth Island Journal.

As you read, consider the following questions:

1. Where does the word "freegan" come from?

2. According to New York City's Department of Sanitation, how many tons of food waste were generated by the city in 2002?

Michael J. Foster, "1,000 Bagels a Night or: How I Learned to Stop Worrying and Love NYC Garbage," *Earth Island Journal*, vol. 23, Spring 2008, p. 64. Copyright 2008 Earth Island Institute. Reproduced by permission.

3. What are some of the activities that the freegan community participates in?

In 2006, I was an intern working with a major conservation organization in one of the most prestigious natural history museums in the world. It was a dream internship, and I, in the spirit of those Broadway musicals I love, felt I was making it in New York City. I was going to survive the Big City, and love doing it. I thrived on the culture, the people, the noise, the work. But I was hungry. While I made enough to pay the rent and have a bit of fun, sometimes I had to go to the local food bank to make sure I had enough to eat. Around Thanksgiving, I had run out of money and food. Looking online I read about the "Really, Really Free Market," and decided to check it out. There I met freegans (a word mash of "free" and "vegan") who were serving free food, and I thought, "This is great!" But where did these people find all this food? The pies, broccoli, carrots, peanut butter, and whole wheat spelt bread? I was soon to find out.

Consumerism Is a Choice

Two or three times a month, my freegan friends and I walk the streets of New York foraging urban food waste. New York City is a land of waste. In 2002, according to the city's Department of Sanitation, New York generated 832,590 tons of food waste. Freegans have figured out a way to recover these lost calories, and by doing so we have made our actions into protest and education. By bringing what was once left for waste back into the material stream, we protest the corporations who steal the commons (such as air and water) used in production processes, define those natural goods as private property, and then discard those resources without regard for the consequences. Because we scavenge visibly and without embarrassment, we demonstrate to others that they can choose to opt out of capitalism. We are showing that consumerism is a choice, not something we are coerced into doing.

The Benefits of Capitalism

Capitalism is relatively new in human history. Prior to capitalism, the way people amassed great wealth was by looting, plundering and enslaving their fellow man. Capitalism made it possible to become wealthy by serving your fellow man. Capitalists seek to find what people want and produce and market it as efficiently as possible.

Walter Williams, "Capitalism and the Common Man,"
Capitalism Magazine, *October 26, 2003.*

The freegan community is loose and without hierarchy, a community that shares with each other and strangers in need. We meet regularly to cook our finds, inviting friends and family to join us. We often provide materials to Food Not Bombs, or other social or political gatherings. These special times help solidify bonds of caring and support.

For me, opening each garbage bag is a wonderful surprise. You'd probably be surprised at what I've found: twenty tofu steaks, sell-by date three weeks from now; ten tubs of yogurt, sell-by date tomorrow; broccoli with one sad spear and four richly green stalks; a five-pound sack of turnips; a case of somewhat brown but delicious bananas; five bags of Oreos. On cold nights, I've found ice cream. There is a yuckiness factor to the smell of mixed materials, and the slip of unnamed liquid that sometimes runs along the sides of a garbage bag is unpleasant to touch. But I have never encountered a rat or roach. I sort through a store's garbage soon after it is placed on the corner. My garbage is fresh and local.

Irrational System of Waste

My favorite stop, and one of the reasons I keep coming back for trash, is the bagel shop. The first time I encountered the bagel shop, I was in awe. There were hundreds of bagels, unspoiled with used coffee grounds, so fresh that the bag was still warm. On that cold November night, steam rose from the black bag as a mound of round doughy goodness was revealed—bagels in all flavors, probably made only hours ago and soon after made into "waste." That night I would make them food, and vow never to buy breakfast again.

If you have ever been to New York, you know how many bagel shops there are—and thus how many bagels are produced. There must be thousands of bagel shops, tossing out tens of thousands of bagels a day. And still, within the city, there are thousands of hungry men, women, and children.

I have a full-time job now, and earn a decent salary. But I continue to be a freegan, not because I have to, but because when I reflect on my choices as a consumer and a capitalist supporter, I have to ask myself three things: What does my consumption cost? What are its negative externalities? What other choices can I make?

I was driven to garbage because of temporary poverty. It was a rational choice prompted by the irrational system of waste that I still observe all around me. In making that choice, I started on a journey toward a different way of living. The journey has most obviously brought me food. More importantly, it has brought me friends.

"*Belt-tightening seems to have . . . prompted a reconsideration of what is acceptable consumerism even for those relatively unaffected by the economic cataclysm.*"

The Recession Is Hurting Consumerism

Alex Williams

In the following viewpoint, Alex Williams asserts that conspicuous consumption is going out of style—even among those who still can afford it—because of the global economic downturn that began in 2008. He contends that sales at high-end retailers plunged and the market for luxury goods has grown softer. The thriftiness of the Great Depression era, which touched the wealthy, may even be making a comeback, the author suggests. Moreover, Williams continues, executives of upscale companies predict that their industries will shift to period of "subtle luxury," wherein ostentation and "bling bling" are out. Williams is a writer for The New York Times.

As you read, consider the following questions:

1. How does Williams support his claim that the sales of luxury goods are declining?

2. What has become fashionable among socialites in New York City, as described by the author?

3. In the author's view, how are luxury handbags changing?

The owners of the South City Grill restaurants in New Jersey opened the first of three planned upscale steakhouses this year [in 2008] and the décor was one of opulence and glamour. The owners "wanted it to sparkle like jewelry," recalled Anurag Nema, one of the designers.

The interior featured shimmering silk curtains, ruby-tinted glass and a hulking crystal chandelier. The stainless steel accents were polished to mirror brilliance, said Nema, who designed the steakhouse South City Prime, in Little Falls, with Orit Kaufman.

The second restaurant is scheduled to open in January [2009] in Montvale, New Jersey, but the sparkle is gone, the designers said. With the economy in free fall, the concept is now sturdy American grill and the name is now Wildfire by South City.

Wooden shutters and brick have replaced the silk curtains. Salvaged wood from a barn will stand in for the ruby-tinted glass. As for the chandelier, well, there is no chandelier.

"There's a shift to get away from glitz," Kaufman said. "I'm almost starting to feel that luxury is a dirty word."

In Poor Taste

It is no secret that consumers are cutting back, anxious about jobs, plummeting home values and shrinking retirement savings. But that belt-tightening seems to have also prompted a reconsideration of what is acceptable consumerism even for those relatively unaffected by the economic cataclysm.

When just about everyone is making do with less, sometimes much less, those $2,000 logo-laden handbags and Aspen vacations can seem in poor taste. "Luxe" is starting to look as out of fashion as square-toed shoes.

As sales at high-end stores like Neiman Marcus plunged by nearly 30 percent in October [2008], compared with a year earlier, Costco sales slipped just 1 percent and Wal-Mart reported gains.

Henri Barguirdjian, the president of Graff, the diamond merchant, said on the cable news channel CNBC last week [in November 2008] that the market for pieces from $20,000 to $100,000 had grown softer. Marine Products, an Atlanta-based maker of yachts and pleasure boats, saw net sales decrease by nearly 40 percent in the quarter ending in September [2008] compared with a year earlier.

"The era of conspicuous consumption, at least for the foreseeable future, has come to a close," said Paco Underhill, the author of *Why We Buy*, which explores the science of retail. "Consumption will still happen. It's just not going to be as public."

He cited a story from an Audi dealer: A buyer of an S4 high-performance sedan requested the nameplate be removed, "so only the person who really knew what they were looking at," he said, "would know what it is."

Today, bejeweled fashionistas are pegged as tone-deaf Marie Antoinettes [France's eighteenth-century queen]. "It's not good taste in our business to walk into a party loaded with the biggest diamonds you can find," said Bud Konheim, the chief executive of Nicole Miller. "You don't brag about paying $10,000 for a dress for a party. The feeling now is, so what are you telling us? You're either a sucker or showing off when people have lost jobs."

The United States Has Been Through Declines in Consumer Spending

Conspicuous consumption has gone out of style before, in the recession that followed the 1980s stock market boom; and briefly after Sept. 11, 2001, until spending was recast as patriotic. But for a precedent for such a complete about-face in people's attitudes toward luxury, you would have to look to the Great Depression. In 1932, wary of insulting the vast number of unemployed Americans, J.P. Morgan Jr. kept his 343-foot, or 105-meter, yacht, *Corsair IV*, in the boatyard, Ron Chernow wrote in *The House of Morgan*.

Among those who remained solvent in the Depression, there was "a widespread sense that you don't flaunt your success," said David Kyvig, the author of *Daily Life in the United States, 1920–1940: How Americans Lived Through the Roaring Twenties and the Great Depression.*

The economic collapse was also seen as a chance, after the 1920s bacchanalia [drunken orgy], for moral cleansing. The industrialist Andrew Mellon said it would "purge the rottenness out of the system. People will work harder, live a more moral life."

Konheim of Nicole Miller, who was born in 1935, said he grew up in a mansion on Long Island, New York, with servants, but even for his family, waste was bad form.

"We had three cars, and they were all Plymouths," he said. "When the soap got down to slivers, what you did was squeeze soap together to make a soap bar—you didn't throw it out."

Today, such thriftiness might make a comeback, said Alexandra Lebenthal, president of the wealth management firm Lebenthal and a contributing editor for the Web site *New York Social Diary*. It has become fashionable, she said, for socialites to talk enthusiastically about sample sales, eBay bargains and postponements at the hair salon in the interests of thrift.

"It's now chic to cut back," she said. "If you ask people if they are going away for the holidays, they say, 'No, we're just

Ways to Be a Recessionista

New hairdo	New parting
New furniture	An upholstery evening class
A weekly manicure	Nails Inc's long-lasting manicure
eBay.com	freecycle.org
Having it all	Having to choose the one, utterly perfect thing you just have to have this month
Investing in a new-season Gucci folk dress	Wearing a skinny jumper [sweater] under a summer smock
A new cashmere scarf	Joining a knitting group

Ruby Warrington, "50 Ways to Be a Recessionista,"
Sunday Times (UK), October 19, 2008.

spending a very quiet holiday with family' instead of 'We're going to Anguilla for Thanksgiving.'"

Harry Slatkin, the founder of Slatkin & Co., a home fragrances company, said he and his wife, Laura, recently canceled a 50th birthday party for her at a Four Seasons hotel. Instead, they plan to have a party at home, with defrosted White Castle cheeseburgers served on silver trays. "It's not time to have splashy birthday parties," Slatkin said. "It's a time to stay home, spend time with friends and connect."

Harrison Group, a market research firm in Waterbury, Connecticut, recently did a survey of attitudes toward wealth among people with household discretionary incomes above $100,000, in partnership with American Express Publishing. While 83 percent of respondents said they were in "good shape to endure this economic climate," those who agreed that "a few luxuries are important in tough times" slipped to 50 percent, from 61 percent, from June to September [2008].

"The definition of living well is changing," said Jim Taylor, a Harrison vice chairman. "There is a desire to not stand out. If you're laying people off, you don't want to buy a Ferrari."

Julien Tornare, a president of the Swiss luxury watchmaker Vacheron Constantin, predicted that his industry would move toward a period of "subtle luxury."

"I think people are going to go with more conservative, not ostentatious—something more discreet that only the connoisseur would know and appreciate, not the bling bling," he said.

Beneficiaries of False Wealth

The rich were not the only ones consuming conspicuously in recent years, said Marshal Cohen, chief industry analyst for NPD Group. The middle class, bingeing on cheap credit, also treated itself. Sub-Zero refrigerators, $300 jeans and Cadillac Escalades seemed within reach, even in average homes. "Those consumers were beneficiaries of false wealth, and they were living, literally, like millionaires," Cohen said.

Now as the middle class goes back to living like the middle class, Cohen said, the culture itself might feel more modest. Consumers may put a premium on comfort over flash. At restaurants, for example, ostentatious fare may look less tempting, said Bobby Flay, the chef and television personality.

"Not to take anything away from chefs who specialize in edible paper, pea shoots and fennel pollen," Flay said, "but I think classic American dishes with substance are what people will grasp onto."

In other words, roast chicken will be very popular.

While fashion is always headed in three directions, consumers are turning away from disposable style—the overdesigned "it" handbag, for example—toward high-quality pieces that will endure over multiple seasons, said David Wolfe, creative director of the Doneger Group, which forecasts fashion and retail trends.

The British company Mulberry has seen a shift toward its unadorned handbags, said Sarah Geary, its marketing director. Until a few months ago, consumer tastes were "focused on extravagance, irrespective of price," she said in an e-mail message, but "in the coming months, the mood will be against that 'blind consumption.'"

Any new era of no-frills consumption, however, might last only as long as it takes for the Dow to recover, which could take months, years or decades.

But Konheim recalled that after the Depression ended, conspicuous consumption was still vaguely sinful. When he was in high school in 1949, for instance, a girl at his school received a mink coat for her Sweet 16 party.

"The whole town was in shock," he said. "It was just a different atmosphere in the entire country."

> "No doubt, people are scared and spending less, but the outlook for consumption going forward is substantially better."

The Recession Will Not Hurt Consumerism

Zachary Karabell

In 2008, the mortgage crisis placed the U.S. financial system in peril, and the nation entered a recession. In the following viewpoint, Zachary Karabell claims that Americans' spending habits are not changing for the worse and that these fears are overblown. For instance, he claims that some increases in personal savings were not due to frugality, but to lower tax payments and higher Social Security payments. This rise in disposable income is bolstered by decreasing energy prices, zero inflation, and falling retail and real estate prices, Karabell adds. He concludes that American consumers are better positioned to lead the way to financial recovery than battered Wall Street. Karabell is president of RiverTwice Research, which specializes in political and economic analysis.

As you read, consider the following questions:

1. How does Karabell support his assertion that workers' unemployment fears are exaggerated?

2. How have credit card debts and auto loans been affected by the recession, according to Karabell?

3. How does Karabell respond to investors' and the government's concerns about credit card defaults?

As the equity markets take another huge step down, it's assumed that American consumers are so shell-shocked by their loss of wealth in both homes and stocks that they will continue to hoard what little cash they have. Yet the relentless negativity about the state of the American consumer may well be overblown. Consumers didn't begin this crisis, but they may very well end it.

It doesn't seem that way right now. In a spate of polls in recent weeks, somewhere between half and two-thirds of all Americans say that they are worried that they will lose their jobs. That fear seems to gain more traction with each passing month, especially with payrolls shrinking as rapidly as they did this month [March 2009] with 651,000 jobs lost and the unemployment rate spiking to 8.1 percent. And as more people fear for the economic future, they have continued to pare their spending, which has in turn deepened the economic downturn.

The fear is real, but is it merited? For starters, it's worth noting that unemployment figures always lag behind economic recovery. No one knows how many more jobs will be lost, but even the most pessimistic estimates assume unemployment will top out at 10.5 percent. Let's say it gets worse and goes to 12 percent, which would mean about 5 million more jobs lost. It's a big number, but that is out of a workforce of about 155 million people in a country with 300 million people. Even if 5 percent more will lose their jobs, surveys shows that more than 50 percent fear that they will. Clearly there is a wide gap between fear and reality.

Long-Term Positive Consequences

How much one worries is subjective. If I told you that there was a 1-in-20 chance of something bad happening to you, would you radically alter your behavior to account for that? That is precisely what is happening, and it is having both short-negative and long-term positive consequences.

The most obvious consequence is that consumers are saving, rapidly. Personal savings jumped from under zero in the middle of 2008 to 3.9 percent in December to 5 percent in January [2009]—almost equal to the 30-year average of 5.6 percent. Critics were quick to point out that some of the increase was due not to frugality but lower tax payments and higher Social Security payments. While there are problems with how the personal-savings rate (not to mention the unemployment rate) is calculated, there's little doubt that people have been socking away money and paying down debt. Outstanding credit-card debt has been decreasing for the past two months [January to March 2009], at least, and plunging auto sales are partly attributable to the unwillingness of many to incur new auto loans. Clearly, consumers are already rebuilding their own balance sheets.

Not only has disposable income been rising, but consumer-spending power has been boosted by lower energy prices and zero inflation. And as retail and real-estate prices fall, every dollar earned can now purchase a larger array of goods and services.

Bears say that these are blips compared to recent wealth destruction. The sky-high price of homes and stocks more than compensated for paltry savings in boom times, and somewhat higher savings now hardly compensate for plummeting personal wealth. Yet having a home go down in price, even if it goes below the sale price, doesn't usually change your

Recession-Chic

Recession-chic advice isn't for the people who actually need it. It's for the people who put their summer homes on the market, not those who've lost the only home they had. . . . And when it comes down to it, if you need to be told that packing your lunch saves money, you're probably not someone who needs to pack your lunch. So please don't pretend that you are.

Kelly Marages,
"Kelly Marages: I'm Not Buying into Recession Chic,"
March 19, 2009. www.dallasnews.com.

monthly costs. If you bought a home for $300,000 and have a fixed-rate mortgage and now the home is worth $250,000, you may feel poorer but your payments haven't changed, nor has your income—unless you've lost your job or been hit by catastrophic health-care costs.

Consumers Will Lead the Way to Recovery

No doubt, people are scared and spending less, but the outlook for consumption going forward is substantially better. Investors and Washington are deeply concerned about a wave of credit-card defaults yet to come, but the vast majority of people remain current on the cards—and on their mortgages—and have income to sustain them. J.P. Morgan recently wrote off $3 billion of its $184 billion in Chase credit-cards loans, which is 1.6 percent of its loans. That got all the news, but it's equally true that 98.4 percent of loans are still good.

As the rate of job losses levels off, so too will the fear of job loss, which in turn will give people more room to assess their finances. They will begin to spend modestly and consistently, and spend the incomes they have, using revolving credit to augment their salaries. In spite of an ugly job report, there are signs that the rate of deterioration has stabilized, which is a necessary first step toward a slow recovery. For fear to abate, all that is needed is a less perceived threat of loss.

Most Americans are in better shape than most of Wall Street. Main Street enjoyed fewer of the bubble's benefits, but its residents are better positioned to dust themselves off and move forward. Looking to Wall Street to lead the recovery is ludicrous; its confidence is shattered and its balance sheets wrecked. Even looking to Wall Street to identify the recovery is too much; its analysts are shell-shocked and legitimately fearful for their employment. This time, markets may lag the recovery. Real economic activity, and the steady spending of Main Street will lead the way.

Periodical Bibliography

The following articles have been selected to supplement the diverse views presented in this chapter.

Benjamin R. Barber   "Which Capitalism Will It Be?" *Newsday*, February 22, 2009.

Campaign   "Farewell to Consumerism," July 11, 2008.

Scott Cannon   "Downturn Has Americans Downsizing Their Spending," *Kansas City Star*, May 23, 2009.

Jeff Colvin   "Why the Party's Over," *Fortune*, November 25, 2008.

Economist   "The End of the Affair," November 22, 2008.

Barbara Ehrenreich   "Fall of the American Consumer," *Nation*, March 11, 2008.

Hoo Ban Kee   "The Joys of Shopping," *Malaysia Star*, January 14, 2008.

Amy Novotney   "What's Behind American Consumerism?" *Monitor on Psychology*, July/August 2008.

John O'Kane   "The Filter Up Effect," *Public Record*, May 24, 2009.

Lisa Pryor   "To Do Without Is Divine, but to Want Lovely Things Is Only Human," *Sydney Morning Herald*, August 23, 2008.

Michelle Singletary   "Necessity or Luxury? Please Redefine," *The Washington Post*, May 21, 2009.

James Surowiecki   "Penny-Wise," *New Yorker*, September 27, 2004.

Tom Vanderbilt   "Self-Storage Nation," *Slate*, July 18, 2005.

Is Consumerism a Problem?

Chapter Preface

M odeled after the main street of a typical small town, malls are a part of the landscape of modern America. The first shopping center to be considered a mall is the Northgate Mall in Seattle, Washington. Opened in the spring of 1950, Northgate offered eight hundred thousand square feet of shopping and featured a forty-four-foot-wide walkway. From the 1970s to the 2000s, the number of malls in the United States increased fourfold, from eleven thousand to forty-five thousand. Today, these shopping centers cover up to 5.5 billion square feet. The largest of them, at 2.5 million square feet of retail space, is the Mall of America in Bloomington, Minnesota. Completed in the fall of 1992, the mega-mall has had over 40 million visitors by 2006.

To some critics, malls enable rampant consumerism, and their presence contributes to the demise of cultural and civic life. Political science professor Benjamin R. Barber says, "Compare any traditional town square with a modern suburban mall. In the square, you'll find a school, town hall, library, general store, park, movie house, church, art gallery, and homes—a true neighborhood exhibiting our human diversity as beings who do more than simply consume. But our new town malls are all shopping, all the time."[i] On the contrary, other observers contend that visiting malls can actually engage people in meaningful ways. History professor Jim Farrell states, "Malls are a place where we answer important questions: What does it mean to be human? What are people for? What is the meaning of things? Why do we work? What do we work for? And what, in fact, are we shopping for?"[ii]

Despite the spread of malls throughout cities and suburbs during the last several decades, the last enclosed mall to open

i. *Los Angeles Times*, April 4, 2007.
ii. *One Nation Under Goods: Malls and the Seductions of American Shopping*, 2003.

in the United States was in 2006, the Mall at Turtle Creek in Jonesboro, Arkansas. Furthermore, as the recession of 2008 worsened, thousands of businesses went bankrupt and storefronts were shuttered, and up to one in four malls could be found empty. In the following chapter, the authors debate whether consumerism is a social, environmental, and economic dilemma or a vital facet of American life.

> "Many American parents feel [pressure] to supply their children with goods that ... are somehow linked to their children's happiness and well-being."

Consumerism Harms Children

Kris Berggren

In the following viewpoint, Kris Berggren argues that consumer culture places children and their parents under growing pressure to buy more stuff. Berggren states that businesses spend millions of dollars on marketing and advertising to stoke material desires within children of all ages, in which wearing trendy clothing brands or having the latest gadget is equated with self-worth, popularity, and happiness. The author recommends that parents counter consumerism by teaching their children to recognize genuine needs from manufactured wants and reject a media filled with marketing messages. Berggren is a writer in Minneapolis, Minnesota, and a longtime contributor to National Catholic Reporter.

As you read, consider the following questions:

1. What is "fashion bullying," according to the author?

Kris Berggren, "Kids and Consumerism: Social Justice-Minded Parents Seek Ways to Resist Pressures of Commercial Culture," *National Catholic Reporter*, vol. 44, November 16, 2007, p. 1a(3). Copyright © The National Catholic Reporter Publishing Company, 115 E. Armour Blvd., Kansas City, MO 64111. All rights reserved. Reproduced by permission of National Catholic Reporter. http://nrconline.org.

2. How did Denise Atwood and Rick Conner teach their son the difference between needs and wants, as described by Berggren?

3. In Berggren's view, when can parents engage in consumerism?

The Declaration of Independence, the founding document on which our national sense of identity is grounded, mentions prominently "the pursuit of Happiness" as an essential condition of our American-ness. And to many Americans, that means the pursuit of stuff. One might sum up the aspirations of many Americans in the words of rocker David Lee Roth, "Money can't buy happiness—but it can buy you a big yacht so you can pull right up next to it."

That's funny, but what's not so funny is the pressure that many American parents feel to supply their children with goods that not only clothe their bodies or occupy their time but are somehow linked to their children's happiness and well-being. Here's a perfect example of how some families find the lure of the marketplace irresistible: One misguided mom, profiled in an Oct. 25 [2007] *Wall Street Journal* article on "fashion bullying," had invested heavily in her sixth-grade daughter's prestige by filling the girl's closet with fashionista clothing brands like Juicy Couture, True Religion and Seven for All Mankind, only to see her daughter's popularity quotient nosedive as her pals moved on to other brands. Even the label names seem intended to tease the spiritually deprived American consumer toward false salvation. And if you're still not convinced that consumption is like a national religion, picture this: a bright yellow Hummer with this vanity plate: HE ROSE. I saw it with my own eyes.

Marketing for All Ages

From toddlers to teenagers, marketers know a target when they see one. Designers are unabashedly creating high-priced

collections sported by the likes of Madonna's and David Beckham's kids. Teenagers do tend to crave the coolest cell phones or i-gadgets with the newest features or colors. But even ordinary kids—and little ones at that—can get sucked into branding.

"My children are just starting to request things their friends have that they would like," said Rachel Morris of Minneapolis, who is reluctant to indulge budding consumer desires. "So they are starting to feel pressure. Toy guns, action figures, Game Boys are the kind of things Noah [age 5] wants. For Maggie [age 3], it's Disney princesses." Morris has managed to say no for now.

Though Morris limits her kids' television viewing and won't buy branded clothing, she admits she's tempted to buy stuff she doesn't really need, even if it's something small like the Halloween party game for Noah she bought impulsively at Target, but later realized she could have made herself. She likens in-your-face consumerism to an intravenous drug. "It's there. You can't battle it all day long. You just let it drip in."

Families who manage to resist rampant consumerism tend to be social critics. "I think the sense of consumerism in the American context—being marketed to, made to feel insecure, and then filled up—is really negative and harmful to us as a society," says Juliann McDermott of Minneapolis. She credits her own beliefs to her family's strong values about American privilege and responsibility for the needs of others. *Maryknoll* magazine [a Catholic publication] was prominent reading material in her home. "I learned at an early age that although there were things I wanted, there were many people in the world who had genuine needs. Knowing that has helped me to feel lucky for what I have and to be content living as simply as possible." She and her husband John Alterini, an artist and cabinetmaker, share those values with their daughter, Johanna, 8.

But McDermott says consumerism isn't all bad—people have needs and wants that are met through buying and selling goods. Denise Atwood of Spokane, Wash., agrees that Americans should be accountable to the global community for their consumer practices. "As the largest consuming country in the world we can make a lot of impact by our consuming decisions."

Atwood and her husband, Rick Conner, own Ganesh Himal Trading, a fair-trade import company. With their son, Cameron, 10, they've made numerous trips to Nepal to source the handcrafted goods they buy and sell to about 200 fair-trade stores in North America. Witnessing the vast differences between the American lifestyle and that of the Nepalese people the family has befriended has honed her son's ability to distinguish needs from wants, said Atwood. "He doesn't whine for things. 'Because I have so much,' he says. He sees through other people's eyes how fortunate he is."

Still she recognizes the relativity of how Americans perceive those needs and wants. "I feel all the time I have way too much. For me, everything is relative to the people I work with in Nepal," she explained. "Others' lives may be relative to their coworkers [here]. They may see themselves as having less compared with their coworkers."

In Alpharetta, Ga., an affluent suburb of Atlanta, Jim Mahon, a retired electronics manufacturing sales representative and father of four adult children, teaches 100 eighth graders each week in his Sunday school classes at St. Thomas Aquinas Parish. He helps his students to connect the dots between what goes into their brains—specifically the influence of media, advertising and peer groups—and the choices they make as consumers, as citizens, and as Christian stewards of God's creation.

"I work with them on marketing and advertising," Mahon said. "Millions of dollars are poured into research to figure out how to get you to part with your money. There is nothing wrong with buying something, but don't get sucked into it. In fact I tell them spend your money, it keeps our economy going. But have a reason, don't just do it subconsciously."

Forgoing TV

One way to avoid the impact of mindless marketing messages is obvious: Abstain from the media that deliver them. Half the families interviewed for this article do not watch television. McDermott and Alterini don't, nor do they use the Internet at home, and "none of us knows how to play a video game," said McDermott, a Montessori elementary teacher. "That is probably where we are the most odd as a family," she admitted. And she won't buy brands that are advertised on television, or that bear a store name. But they aren't completely immune to their daughter's desire to fit in with friends; Johanna loves a certain type of T-shirt favored by skateboarders, so when she saw one and told her dad she'd like it, he bought it for her.

It's not surprising that families who forgo TV spend time reading, playing music or sports, or being outdoors. McDermott's family goes to the off-leash dog park weekly.

"Spending time out of doors helps us to combat some of the consumerism. Because you don't need a lot if you are out walking in the woods; clothing is about function, not fashion. It's more about having experiences together than the stuff."

Laurie Powers, a lawyer in Spokane, takes Carter, 11, and twins Fiona and Bridget, 7, to the library each week to stock up on books instead of buying them. "They can see visually; if we were buying all this stuff, we would have books everywhere!" Her children practice karate and soccer together, and take piano lessons. They don't have television, but they do have a GameCube and a Wii game system that Carter paid for himself.

A Practice of Awareness

These parents do give an inch. They know there are times when surviving the daily grind preempts idealistic values. As families' needs shift, they may depend more on conveniences that are less in keeping with their overall values, or conversely they may find time to be more conscientious about their choices.

Powers and her husband, Breean Beggs, also a lawyer, are activists who compost and recycle, serve on committees in the community and at their church, Westminster Presbyterian, and attend events like the Bioneers Conference, an annual gathering of progressives interested in environmental and social justice causes. Yet Laurie recalls, a few years ago the family "went through the McDonald's phase," during an especially hectic period when they were relocating to Spokane, remodeling a home, and juggling two jobs and three children.

"There was a time when that worked for us and that's just what we did. Now we have more time to be more conscious," Laurie said. Today the children are well versed in reduce-reuse-recycle practices and engaged in family decisions such as whether or not to go out to eat or to save the money and resources.

Living one's values is not a zero sum equation, in other words. The meal you finish tonight won't, in fact, immediately prevent a child from starving in Biafra, Iraq, Darfur or Haiti. But choosing not to waste food or to avoid excess packaging or to save money on brand names that you can invest in college savings or donate to charities or even buy fair-traded goods shows your kids you don't have to go with the flow.

Morris sums up her attitude about the daily experience of resisting the consumer machine. "It's really more a practice of awareness. It's a path. I want to be a person who thinks about all the issues that are related. And to know how I can be, at least, not part of the problem."

> "Rather than seriously question the na-
> ture of our consumerist society, we in-
> stead choose to focus anxiety exclusively
> on children."

The Dangers of Consumerism
for Children Are Overstated

Karen Sternheimer

In the following viewpoint excerpted from It's Not the Media:
The Truth About Pop Culture's Influence on Children, *author
Karen Sternheimer declares that fears about consumerism and
children are actually based on the anxieties of adults and parents. Consumption allows a child to step away from parental
control and establish an independent identity. Sternheimer contends that children use consumption to participate within their
own culture and peer groups, just as adults do. So, instead of
controlling what they purchase or shielding them from consumerism, she advises parents and teachers to seek the underlying
meanings products have to their children and teach them to be
critical consumers. Sternheimer is a lecturer in the Department
of Sociology at the University of Southern California.*

As you read, consider the following questions:

1. What example does Sternheimer provide to support her claim that children partake in consumer culture as a social act?

2. What is the key difference between children's consumption and that of adults, in Sternheimer's view?

3. How does the author view consumerism and American culture?

Along with turkey sandwiches and leftovers, the day after Thanksgiving has become associated with a major shopping marathon; at least, that's what retailers hope. The obligatory news reports of crowds eagerly awaiting pre-dawn openings of toy stores return each year as adults do battle to get the hottest toys of the year first. Last year [2002] was no different; the news featured an argument between two parents over "cuts" in line as they waited for the 5 A.M. opening of a Toys"R"Us. At another store a woman was shoved so violently she sustained a black eye.

Stories of out-of-control adult shoppers are common when the holiday buying season starts, but concerns about consumption and advertising usually focus exclusively on children and teens, because many of us believe that they are easily influenced. Fears persist that young people are easily swayed by advertising, will be parted from their (and their parents') money, and are in need of protection from advertisers. But are young people really the naïve consumers we often presume them to be?. . .

Consumption represents a step away from parental control and serves as a way of creating an identity distinct from parents. We will see that concerns about advertising and consumption reflect an ambivalence towards our consumer-driven culture. Rather than seriously question the nature of our consumerist society, we instead choose to focus anxiety exclusively on children. Advertisers speak directly to kids, sometimes working against parents' attempts to curb their material desires. Fears about advertising are based on this perceived intrusion, as well as on the difficulty parents have controlling information their kids get from media sources. . . .

Rethinking Childhood and Consumption

Participating in consumer culture doesn't necessarily mean that children (or adults) are inordinately materialistic. Researcher Ellen Seiter found, in a study of preschool children, that consumption is used to create both group and individual identity. The children wore T-shirts with recognizable logos and carried lunch boxes with Disney characters to create a shared culture and let their peers know that they were "in on" kid culture. I recall that in my own childhood, consumption was used in much the same way. When I was in the third grade, having a mini windup doll called a "kidalong" meant you could play kidalong mom with the other girls. We also bought mini desk organizers with tiny drawers for our desks at school and colorful binders to hold our schoolwork. I chose a green pencil holder and a binder with a plaid cover that at once set me apart and marked my group membership. Consumption is a social act: Buying may be an individual activity, but the types of purchases we make can create a sense of shared identity. Children's play with particular toys or knowing about the latest fad is a way of creating a shared culture. Adults use consumption in the same way, of course, buying cars, gadgets, and clothes that indicate we are members of various groups.

Maybe we should question why consumption is so much a part of fitting in with other kids, but curiously few adults ask the same question about our own behavior, like why we desire a $50,000 car when the $15,000 one works just as well or better. It's too simple to say we are all just fodder for advertising genius. We consume what we do for a number of reasons: We need things, we are making statements about who we are as individuals, and we are affiliating ourselves with certain groups, making status distinctions. Children are no different in this regard.

We therefore need to take caution when we criticize children for exhibiting buying habits similar to our own. The key difference between children's consumption and our own is that as adults we tend to be outsiders in the world of children's culture. Their consumption is an easy target for us because their culture may not hold meaning for us and may even seem silly. Some parents cite the fervor over fads like Pogs or Pokémon as proof that children are easily duped into throwing money away on items adults find useless. [Magazine publisher] Scott Donaton wrote in *Advertising Age* of his disgust after taking his kids to see *Digimon: The Movie*, which he called "an unimaginative wholesale rip-off." I'm not sure what his kids thought, and of course he is entitled to his opinion, but too often adults judge children's culture based on our own tastes. When adults view children's tastes pejoratively it is easy to proclaim that slick advertisers have hoodwinked kids, rather than recognize that children may enjoy things we adults don't get.

Kid culture creates anxieties amongst adults when it becomes apparent that their children's sources of influence have expanded beyond the family. Children's consumption decisions are shaped by peers, teachers, and other adults—no longer do parents have the ability to fully influence their children's tastes. Creating separate identities signifies a loss of control, a wedge between parents and children. Advertising's power is more symbolic than real, but to many parents it signifies a very real loss of power.

Children use consumption to begin to assert their independence from their parents, as being a consumer in American society is a step towards maturity. Cultural anthropologist Cindy Dell Clark found in her interviews with elementary

121

school children and their parents that money left by the "tooth fairy" serves as an important rite of passage. A child may begin to earn an allowance at this age, and thus they learn to become consumers in their own right. Clark notes that this time is often difficult for parents, who must come to terms with the fact that their child's "babyhood" has ended. So while the step towards independence is important, parents may indeed feel a powerful sense of loss that accompanies a child's entrée into the world of consumer culture. Advertisers get blamed for "luring" children out into the world, but within a consumerist society this is in fact an inevitable and in some respects necessary step away from total parental control. Anxiety about young children's consumption coincides with their first steps towards independence and the decreased centrality of their families.

Of course an identity *only* based on consumption is rather empty, and concerns about advertising often stem from the fear that consumption is making this generation more superficial than children of the past. But learning to be a responsible consumer means learning that simply having things will not fill all of our needs. This may be a hard lesson to teach. Yes, in part because advertisers do insist their products will cure what ails us, but more importantly because lots of us have yet to master this lesson ourselves. *Los Angeles Times* fashion writer Valli Herman-Cohen gushed that she "love(s) (her) insanely expensive purse . . . and everything it says about me." Although tongue-in-cheek, the author explained how good it made her feel to buy the deeply "discounted" bag (marked down from $2,000 to a bargain $1,500). At the same time we need to recognize that consumption can be pleasurable—who am I to judge how a person spends $1,500 of her own money? My point here is that we adults haven't done a great job resisting advertisers' claims that a newer new car is the answer or that we can lose ten pounds this weekend by swallowing some magic powder.

These are all serious issues to address in a consumer-oriented society, where we are told by government leaders that if we stop consuming people will lose their jobs and where interest rates are lowered to encourage us to buy things we can't afford and to discourage saving. Yet public discussion tends to focus exclusively on children's consumption and seldom turns a critical eye on advertising for adults. In fact, if adults do question capitalism or our culture of consumption, they tend to be viewed as radical extremists. But adults can safely charge the next generation for being overly materialistic or pawns of advertisers without challenging the status quo. Rather than address consumption head-on, we deflect our concerns onto children and their consumption.

We adults are very much a part of a consumption-oriented society, where we show people we love them with material goods and are asked to shop to show our patriotism. Children are regularly rewarded with gifts and learn that special holidays mean special consumption and that happiness can be found in a store. Consumption is the building block of a capitalist society and has become the hallmark of American culture.

If people have a problem with capitalism and consumption, fine. Just don't leave yourself out of the circle of responsibility: If kids are overly materialistic, it is because the rest of us are.

Critical Consumerism

Instead of simply trying to eliminate children's relationship with consumer culture, I advocate critical consumerism, a mode of behavior that acknowledges that we are part of a consumption-based society. This means admitting that the experience of consumption can be fun and enjoyable but can also be empty and ultimately cannot fill every emotional need, as it often promises.

Children and Advertising

Television can be an important learning tool for children, but it must be used with the greatest care. As part of the television "picture," advertising can provide children with a great deal of information about the world around them. Advertising also may be a child's first introduction to what it means to be a consumer in this economy. Ads can help a child appreciate the diversity of available choices, and how to select wisely from among them. But, it must always be remembered that children need close parental guidance when it comes to advertising.

Ode,
"Teach Your Kids to Be Consumer Conscious,"
April 2008. www.odemagazine.com.

Parents and teachers ought to focus on preparing children to be members of a consumer-driven culture, or, if truly concerned about our consumption-based society, attempt to change the nature of the culture itself. This, of course, is a much more difficult task, since many adults have no intention of changing their own behavior. So rather than continually attempting to shield children from the pervasive culture of consumption, which eventually fails, we should work to create more critical consumers, starting with ourselves.

To do so we must first acknowledge the pleasurable aspects of our own consumption and recognize that children experience the same feelings. This process must be reflective rather than authoritative; people don't want to be told they have bad taste, including children. Adults should move beyond only controlling what children purchase and seek to learn what meaning children give to products. Both adults and children would benefit from challenging the belief that consumption and happiness go hand in hand.

Additionally, we need to understand that advertising is just a piece of a big puzzle, that consumerism is built into the fabric of American economic and cultural life. Trying to safeguard against "premature consumerism" is a tactic that is doomed to fail. Learning to be wise consumers is far more useful than attempting to keep children away from commercial contact.

The Real Fear: Losing Control

The fear of advertising stems from adult ambivalence about the nature of our consumer-based culture, but also from children's power to influence adults. Additionally, children use consumption to create cultural experiences separate from their parents, by aligning their tastes with peers. All of these things represent a loss of adults' control over children's worlds and thus a perceived reduction in adult authority. A child with independent tastes and desires represents a step away from conventional adult power. But rather than recognize the autonomy children may express, we are quick to blame advertisers for imposing "false" needs on children. To deny any influence of marketing and media culture would be naïve, but so too is any view of children that negates the complex process of peer culture and identity in negotiating desire.

Until we deal with the tension created by the imbalance of power between adults and children, advertisers will be able to continue to utilize this tactic to gain the trust and attention of young people. The answer is not to totally eliminate adult authority, but instead to take a closer look at where adult power is used arbitrarily. Discourse that uniformly condemns children as ignorant consumers easily swayed by advertising is one such abuse of power, a sweeping generalization that deepens the rift between generations. Adults cannot legislate taste or identity, nor can we ensure that kids grow up to be exactly whom we hope they become. Both children and adults can be empowered by learning to become more critical and knowledgeable about consumption, but this can't happen with a "you-first" attitude. Adults need to take the lead by examining our own relationship with consumer culture.

> "So although green consumerism appears to represent a rejection of materialism, in practice it is no less preoccupied with buying things than are those brand junkies chasing the latest fashionable product."

The Environmental Movement Has Created Green Consumerism

Frank Furedi

Green consumerism is understood as the ethical, informed consumption of goods and services that are sustainable and environmentally responsible. But in the following viewpoint, Frank Furedi argues that the movement in actuality is fixated on acquiring commodities and brands that enhance social status and identity. He insists that green consumers view their purchases as moral statements that affirm their superiority to consumers who make "evil" choices in food and clothing. Ultimately, the author claims that under green consumerism, everything from carbon emissions to drinking water is commoditized. Furedi is a profes-

Frank Furedi, "The Greening of Capitalism," *spiked*, February 29, 2008. Reproduced by permission. www.spiked-online.com.

sor of sociology at University of Kent in the United Kingdom and author of Politics of Fear, Paranoid Parenting, *and* Culture of Fear.

As you read, consider the following questions:

1. How does Furedi characterize environmentalism?

2. In James Heartfield's opinion, why do environmental capitalists "manufacture scarcity"?

3. How will green ethics affect the marketplace, in Furedi's view?

Possibly the single most important development within Western societies in the past quarter of a century has been the rise and rise of environmentalism.

It's worth recalling that back in the 1970s, earnest, Malthusian[1], 'small is beautiful' advocates lived on the margins of everyday life. As with so many other post-Second World War cultural developments, environmentalism was seen and experienced by many as yet another California-invented fad. Even after the aftermath of the 1970s oil crisis, the miserabilist report [*The*] *Limits to Growth* by the Club of Rome [global think tank] was strongly criticised by serious commentators from both the left and right. The idea of sustainable development had not yet been invented. Classical 'small is beautiful' or 'let's get back to our roots' romantic sentiments competed with numerous other critiques of modern life.

An Environmentalist Imperative

Today, environmentalism dominates Western cultural sensibilities—even though its most avid crusaders keep up the pretence that environmentalism is a brave radical movement, a

---

1. Referring to the theory of Thomas Malthus, population increases at a faster rate than its means of subsistence, and unchecked will lead to widespread poverty and degradation.

David forced to contend with an army of powerful Goliaths. Although greens continually moralise about society's hypocrisy and irresponsibility towards the planet, the fact is that environmentalism dominates the cultural imagination, directly shapes contemporary lifestyle, and has emerged as a powerful moralising project. To be green is to be virtuous, responsible, if not yet holy. Public discourse is underpinned by green values, and for politicians 'helping to save the planet' has become a point-scoring apple-pie issue.

Most importantly, capitalist society appears to be restructuring according to an environmentalist imperative. Even hard-headed capitalist entrepreneurs have opted for business plans underpinned by an environmentalist ethos. Of course, some entrepreneurs have a healthy cynicism about the merits of fashionable envirobabble, but nevertheless they understand that they cannot thrive unless they talk the talk.

British commentator James Heartfield has written a thought-provoking essay that attempts to make sense of what drives the ascendancy of Green Capitalism. The main merit of the essay is that it endeavours to explain what appears to be a new phase in the cultural and economic life of capitalism. In particular, Heartfield is rightly preoccupied with trying to find an answer to one of the key questions of our time: Why has capitalism come to embrace restraint and the ethos of sustainability, when as an economic system it has always been characterised by its commitment to raise productivity and expand production?

The strength of Heartfield's *Green Capitalism* is its critique of green consumerism. In a well-argued section, Heartfield argues that the outward expression of anti-consumerism tends to coexist with a new obsessive fixation on the act of consumption. So although green consumerism appears to represent a rejection of materialism, in practice it is no less preoccupied with buying things than are those brand junkies chasing the latest fashionable product. Arguably, as Heartfield implies, shopping means more to green consumers than it does to the shallow brand-fixated consumers they so despise. For a start, green consumers imagine that their purchases are meaningful ethical acts. 'Ethical shopping flatters us that our everyday buying is doing good', argues Heartfield.

Such ethical transactions represent a form of 'status affirmation'. And as is the case with all forms of status affirmation, these green shopping habits are acts of social demarcation. Through adopting the identity of an ethical shopper, someone who cares and who reflects on what they purchase, green consumers are self-consciously marking themselves off from their moral, and incidentally their *social*, inferiors. Their denunciation of their fellow human beings who wear trashy throwaway cheap clothes and eat cheap food is a modern-day version of the paternalistic lectures made by Victorian do-gooders.

Ironically, green protest against consumerism doesn't represent the rejection of consumption, but rather its moralisation. From a sociological perspective, green consumption can be seen as a new form of conspicuous consumption. This is consumption for effect. Consumption apparently must no longer be an impulsive act of buying—rather it has become a massively over-examined experience, and both a moral statement and an affirmation of status and identity. In the nineteenth century, theories of commodity fetishism noted the growing tendency for people to live through things—commodities appeared to acquire a life of their own through the working of the market. In the world of green consumerism, the fetish of commodities acquires an unprecedented significance. Things are assigned human and ethical significance. Thus we have the stigmatisation of certain foods as 'evil' and, the rendering of other products as 'ethical'.

Engineering Scarcity

Green Capitalism also makes some interesting observations about the growing valuation of scarcity in twenty-first century

Western culture. Heartfield writes of an 'economy of wasting time', where resources are devoted to initiatives that make little sense except as rituals of ethical intent, such as recycling. He discusses an apparent trend towards reversing the division of labour through the idealisation of subsistence, small-scale and decentralised activities. Heartfield believes that these trends are the outcome of a process that he calls 'manufactured scarcity', and that capitalism has become reoriented around reaping benefits from deindustrialisation. It appears that 'the cannier green capitalists worked out' that 'scarcity increases price' and 'manufacturing scarcity can increase returns', he argues. Yet while this analysis of scarcity provides some interesting insights into the workings of the market, it is also the weak link in *Green Capitalism*.

It is always tempting to interpret contemporary reality as an inevitable outcome of purposeful forces. Often when examining the present, we feel tempted to read history backwards and place far too much emphasis on the element of subjective intent. To some extent, *Green Capitalism* moves in this direction and discusses today's green economy as the outcome of a project initiated by capitalism itself.

In an attempt to substantiate this point, Heartfield claims that it was the 'elite industrialists of the Club of Rome' who commissioned the report *The Limits to Growth* and who were also responsible for encouraging the rise of the modern environmental movement. Furthermore, he claims that the conversion of the children of many of these industrialists to environmentalism demonstrates that this was a project initiated by Big Business. Of course, few would question that the modern environmentalist movement has elitist origins. But the business world should not be endowed with the foresight and the power to launch a project in the 1970s whose objectives would only be realised decades later. Back in the 1970s, the Club of Rome reflected a general sense of malaise, but it did not express the agenda of Western capitalism. After the Club of

The Myth of Green Capitalism

The most alarming aspect of the corporate assault on environmentalism is that many environmentalists have swallowed the myth of green capitalism.

In a 1990 *Chain Reaction* article, academic Tim Doyle analysed the consolidation of a "professional elite" within the environment movement and its co-option by government and industry.

Doyle warned, "If these trends of elite dominance continue . . . then the politicians, the government bureaucracy and the developers will have complete control over the movement's political agenda and its terms of reference. The time dimension; the rules of the game; the extent of the trade-offs; the sources of money; the mutual personnel: all these factors will be defined by the dominant regime."

Doyle's warning is as relevant today as it was [in 1990]. An important aspect of the struggle to save the environment is to reject the green capitalist illusions of leaders of the environment movement . . . especially since they now speak the same language as the corporate polluters.

Jim Green,
"The Illusion of Green Capitalism,"
Green Left Online, *June 9, 1999.*

Rome, the vast majority of business leaders continued to be devoted to growth and regarded environmental issues as being of marginal significance. The greening of capitalism occurred later, and it was the product of complex cultural and social interactions in a world where defenders of the market economy found it difficult to give meaning to their activities.

Heartfield's focus on intentionally engineered scarcity may prove to be misplaced. It is based upon the premise that the rationing of goods is a principal feature of capitalism. Heartfield argues that 'capitalism was from the outset a system of rationing' and that it 'cannot exist without scarcity', for 'scarcity is capitalism's system of control'. This association of scarcity with capitalism is not very helpful. Every society so far has been in part a system of rationing, and arguably rationing is one of the *least* distinctive features of capitalism. Similarly, every society so far has been associated with scarcity, too, so in one sense it seems obvious that none of these societies could have existed without scarcity.

But can the engineering of scarcity, as Heartfield suggests, become the driver of contemporary economic life? Individual entrepreneurs have often attempted to corner markets, create artificial shortages and enjoy the benefits of monopoly prices. However, what works for a relatively short period of time for the individual capitalist cannot overcome the force of competition. On occasion, competitors can make agreements to divide up the market, but in the end such attempts soon tend to break down under pressure of market forces.

The Creation of New Demands

What *Green Capitalism* characterises as the 'engineering of scarcity' could be more usefully described as the creation of new demands. Indeed, what is most striking today is not simply the rise of the celebration of scarcity, but the growing tendency to marketise every aspect of life. Under the banner of green capitalism, more and more features of economic life are being reorganised and restructured. Everything from the emission of carbon to the air we breathe to the water we drink has been transformed into a commodity. Arguments for protecting nature are really a demand for the gradual securitisation of the environment. Powerful forces insist on transforming every object of possible use into a value, in an attempt to subject them all to the influence of market transactions. Yes, resources are wasted on 'sustainable technology' and on rituals of green morality—but communities have always 'wasted' resources on building pyramids, palaces, temples and a variety of white elephant projects.

James Heartfield does an excellent job of alerting us to the importance of the economic reorganisation that is taking place under the environmentalist imperative. But it is far from clear to what extent this process represents a new dynamic towards the construction of scarcity. It is useful to recall that capitalism is continually reorganising its method of production and the way it relates to the market. Frequently it undermines what it achieved in the past, but through an act of 'creative destruction' it tries to restore profitability and guarantee itself a new phase of accumulation. Paradoxically, it may well be that green ethics will provide the market with unprecedented opportunities to expand consumption through the creation of new demands that are harmonious with the status-conscious but very conspicuous and ethically-addicted consumer. *Green Capitalism* provides an important point of departure for thinking about the future.

| "We need to rethink the way we define a strong economy to encompass not only the health of our financial markets, but also the health of our natural resources."

Rejecting Consumerism Can Help the Environment

Wendee Holtcamp

*In the following viewpoint, Wendee Holtcamp recounts her experience of only buying secondhand goods for thirty days, which she states reduced her ecological impact and promoted her understanding of consumerism. Holtcamp claims that the American consumer lifestyle creates tremendous waste, which is partly owed to corporations that manufacture and market goods that are designed to wear out or become obsolete in a short period of time. Buying used, she maintains, takes restraint and creativity, but lessens the use of dwindling raw materials and challenges throwaway consumption. The author is an environmental writer and journalist and has contributed to magazines such as Na*tional Wildlife *and* Sierra.

Wendee Holtcamp, "My 30 Days of Consumer Celibacy," *OnEarth*, Summer 2007. Reproduced by permission. www.onearth.org.

As you read, consider the following questions:

1. What did the Compacters intend to do, as described by the author?

2. According to the viewpoint, what would be the consequences of widespread secondhand shopping on the economy?

3. Which consumer goods have relatively small environmental impact, as stated by Holtcamp?

For a whole month, one writer practiced a kind of abstinence so she could better understand her own complicity in our throwaway culture. It wasn't easy.

A few days into a vow of shopping celibacy, I visit a Hallmark store with my kids. The 75-percent-off rack draws me in. I've forgotten that I'm supposed to be living according to the Compact, an agreement to avoid all new purchases in favor of used goods in an attempt to reduce my impact on the environment.

"Look at these cute penguins," I say, showing them to my kids.

My 10-year-old son, Sam, picks one up. "Cool. They poop candy."

I pay and leave the store before realizing what I've done. I stop short. "I am not supposed to buy anything new!" I yelp. My kids glare at me. "Well," I say, taking a deep breath, "I will just have to start again tomorrow."

The original Compacters, who formed their group in early 2006, did not intend to start a movement. It was just 10 San Francisco friends trying to reduce their consumption by not buying new stuff for a year. The group's manifesto was simple: to counteract the negative global environmental and socioeconomic impacts of U.S. consumer culture. Named after the Pilgrims' revolutionary Mayflower Compact, the small idea led to a Yahoo! Web site that has attracted more than 8,000 adherents and spawned some 50 groups in spots as far-flung as Hong Kong and Iceland.

What they don't say on the Compact Web site: Kicking consumerism may require its own 12-step program. So after my Hallmark relapse, I started again from square one. According to the guidelines, I must buy used, or borrow. No new stuff, with the exception of food, necessary medicines and health care items, and—no joke—underwear.

"This all started over a dinner conversation about the limitations of recycling," says Rachel Kesel, a professional dog walker and one of the original friends who established the Compact. What else could people do to tread more lightly on the earth? "One of the solutions is not to buy so much crap."

The Trashiest Country

The average American generates about 4.5 pounds of trash a day—a figure that, according to the Environmental Protection Agency, includes paper, food, yard trimmings, furniture, and everything else you toss out at home and on the job. That makes the United States the trashiest country in the industrialized world, followed by Canada at 3.75 pounds a day and the Netherlands at 3 pounds a day. In part, we can thank the corporations that spend billions to convince us that the newest, shiniest widgets will make us happy and attract friends and lovers. What's more, each new widget is designed to wear out or otherwise fade into obsolescence, so we'll have almost no choice but to buy more and more. In the words of Dr. Seuss's Once-ler in *The Lorax*, "A Thneed's a Fine-Something-That-All-People-Need!!" The old Thneed—often in working condition—goes out with the trash. And in the process of making thneeds, the Swomee-Swans get smog in their throats and the Super-Axe-Hacker whacks all the Truffala-Trees, and the gills of the Humming-Fish get gummed up with Gluppity-Glup.

I was already an eco-savvy consumer when I began my moratorium on new stuff. I bought organic produce, "green" beauty products, compact fluorescent lightbulbs, and the like. "A month won't be too bad," I told my preteen daughter. Without thinking I added, "I'll just buy everything I need beforehand." She laughed. As if I were joking.

The Compact has, for the most part, attracted people who were already living frugally or eco-consciously and whose dismay over society's overzealous buying habits may have been brewing for some time. Such feelings are not universally shared. On a Seattle radio show that aired just after the group formed, the host ripped into John Perry, one of the original Compacting friends, saying, "You people are bad for America and you're bad for the American economy."

A Web forum mocking the Compact sprang up, one of the first posts proclaiming, "Today I'm starting a Compact wherein no one can buy anything yellow. Except bananas. And lemons. . . . Oh, wait. I need legal pads." The Compact founders were called pretentious, since they live upper-middle-class lives, and hypocritical, since one of them works in marketing—the art and science of selling goods.

After this criticism, the Compacters consulted several economists about the soundness of their premise. Alex Tabarrok, a professor of economics at George Mason University, theorizes that if throngs of citizens shopped secondhand, it would drive the market to produce higher-quality, more durable goods. Some sectors of the economy would expand, he says, as people spent more money on services or used goods, which are often sold by smaller, independent business owners. But if enough of us started buying less stuff, wouldn't corporate profits fall, leading to layoffs and a drop in the gross domestic product—that classic index of the economy?

I ran this by Bob Costanza, a professor of ecological economics at the University of Vermont who has given some thought to the question. "If 'growing GDP' is considered to be the goal, then yes, buying secondhand will hurt 'the economy' because less stuff will be produced per unit time," he says. "But this just shows how wrong this narrow conception of the economy is." So maybe we need to rethink the way we define a strong economy to encompass not only the health of our financial markets, but also the health of our natural resources.

Still, not everyone immediately grasps why buying used products has less impact on the environment than buying new ones. When you buy a new widget—a cell phone, for example—the store orders a replacement, instigating a chain of events that eventually leads to more raw material being mined from the earth. In contrast, when you buy used, the seller—at a garage sale, a thrift store, or on eBay—does not put in a replacement order. The chain stops there. I nearly lost a friend once when I bought a used teak table after I had exhorted her never to buy anything that wasn't made from sustainably harvested wood. My purchase did not cause a living tree to be cut down, I told her. She didn't get it.

Giving up new stuff forced me to shop creatively. A visit to Goodwill yielded a travel mug for my Starbucks visits, clothes for my daughter, and a bongo drum to substitute for the practice pad my son needed for his drum lessons. Buying a basketball net proved more challenging. I found one through Freecycle, a Web site where users trade belongings, but it had so much rust it wouldn't have passed muster with my suburban homeowners' association. After much looking, I bought a like-new one for $30 on my local Craigslist Web site. Then it took two weeks and 55 e-mail, text, and voice messages before I got my basketball net.

When my laptop went on the fritz, I panicked. I needed a working computer, so I went shopping for a new one. This time, the widget-maker's plan to lure me into buying the newest, shiniest model backfired. Microsoft's new Windows Vista operating system won't work with the perfectly good computer accessories I already own, so if I were to fork over a

Consumers Are Moving in a Sustainable Direction

Using their market muscle, consumers are already helping to drive interest in green products of all kinds. Sales of Toyota's hybrid vehicles, for example, jumped from 18,000 in 1998 to 312,500 in 2006 and now number more than 1 million worldwide. Sales of compact fluorescent lightbulbs (CFLs) in the United States alone totaled 100 million in 2005. And purchases of organic foods worldwide jumped by 43 percent between 2002 and 2005, to $43 billion. Impressive as the growth in green products has been, sales constitute just a small share of the consumption of each product line—U.S. sales of CFLs accounted for only 5 percent of lightbulb sales in 2007, and organic agriculture is practiced on less than 1 percent of global agricultural land. Given that consumption accounts for a large share of the GDP [gross domestic product] of most economies—in the United States in 2006 it was 70 percent—consumers are barely tapping their power to swing economies in a sustainable direction. They need help.

Gary Gardner and Thomas Prugh,
"Chapter 1: Seeding the Sustainable Economy,"
State of the World 2008:
Innovations for a Sustainable Economy. 2008.
www.worldwatch.org.

grand for a new laptop, I'd also have to buy new software, new drivers, and new Microsoft Office programs. Exasperated, I took a deep breath and went home. Sticking to my Compact vow, I hauled an old dinosaur of a computer out of the closet while I waited, impatiently, for laptop repairs.

I wondered: Am I really making a difference? Do I need to eliminate everything I would ordinarily buy new? The answer surprised me. In *The Consumer's Guide to Effective Environmental Choices*, Michael Brower and Warren Leon of the Union of Concerned Scientists calculated the impact of various consumer purchases on four environmental problem areas: air pollution, water pollution, global warming, and habitat alteration. They analyzed the environmental footprints of everything from cheese to carpet to feminine products and then aggregated them into 50 categories of goods and services. In the end, they found that just 7 of the 50 categories were responsible for the lion's share of environmental degradation: cars and trucks; meat and poultry farming; crop production; home heating, hot water, and air conditioning; household appliances; home construction; and household water use and sewage treatment.

Interestingly, the personal items I worked so hard to forgo are not among the worst offenders. Clothing, books, magazines, and toys account for a relatively small fraction of the total environmental destruction wrought by our modern lifestyle. Brower and Leon suggest that we focus on choices that matter most: alternative energy utility providers, energy-saving appliances, organic food, and fuel-efficient or hybrid cars. Over time, buying smart may be more important than buying used.

I grew up in a log cabin with a hippie dad who chose simplicity. We had an outhouse, wood stoves, chickens, and a vegetable garden. Compacting should be second nature to me. Still, I found myself rebelling. I'm a self-employed single mom! Call me an impatient American consumer, but the truth is, I both care passionately about the environment and live in a world where I often have zero extra time. And shopping for used stuff takes lots of time. I made a commitment some time ago to use my purchasing power to help the environment, and spending a month Compacting forced me to reexamine my priorities. It also helped me reconsider my needs versus my wants. We could have forgone the candy-pooping penguins, and I can find many perfectly good things used—and at less cost. But eventually, I will need a brand new laptop.

"I don't think everyone has to stop shopping to change American consumption habits," Rachel Kesel tells me. "But a lot of people need to be put on detox for a while."

| "Credit—or, perhaps more accurately, debt—seems to be there for the asking."

Credit Card Consumerism Creates Debt

Stuart Vyse

In the following viewpoint excerpted from Going Broke: Why Americans Can't Hold on to Their Money, *Stuart Vyse states that American consumers are accumulating huge balances on their credit cards that they are struggling to pay. Drawing from personal examples, Vyse argues that credit card debt is not necessarily the consequence of lavish spending, but happens when credit is used to cover increasing costs of living. Between media messages of materialism and the good life, credit is even offered to those without incomes, like college students, and those already deep in debt. Vyse is a professor of psychology at Connecticut College.*

As you read, consider the following questions:

1. What happens to debtors after periods of delinquency and nonpayment, as described by Vyse?

2. What example does Vyse provide to support his claim that credit card companies make it easy for holders to go into debt?

3. According to the author, which category of people who go through bankruptcy courts are the largest?

I was a college professor; my wife was a social worker. We lived in a modest house in a neighborhood that was a mixture of blue- and white-collar families. I rarely bought clothes, and our kids went to public schools. We thought of ourselves as solidly middle-class—even upper-middle-class—but somehow we were sinking. Yes, we had a house and young children, but at this stage in our careers, life seemed much harder than it was supposed to be. Every decision we made was tinged with anxiety and worry about where the money was going to come from. We never felt comfortable.

Then came the divorce.

In January 1999, my wife and I began the process of dissolving our twenty-year marriage. Soon I moved out of the house and began paying child support, but there were also thousands of dollars in attorney's fees and other settlement expenses. Because we agreed that she would keep the house until our daughter, who was seven, entered middle school, I had to start over again in an apartment with few of the furnishings my new life would require. I entered this period with approximately $7,000 in unsecured credit card debt. I was driving a twelve-year-old Toyota Corolla I had purchased used. All my previous school and automobile loans had been paid off, but now I was forced to take out a $4,000 loan to cover mounting divorce costs. My credit card balance started to grow.

Four years later, in the summer of 2003, my world had regained some stability. The loan for divorce expenses was paid off, and I was paying all my bills on time. My children had adapted well to traveling between their mother's house and my apartment. By necessity, I was living rather frugally, but my children and I had what we needed. There was just one remaining problem: my MBNA MasterCard, the only bank card I was carrying at the time, had a balance of $12,000. In relation to the funds I had available to support myself—after child support and taxes were taken out—this unsecured debt represented 30 percent of my net annual income. When I looked back, I knew my life had not been particularly lavish or undisciplined, but somehow I found myself among those Americans who are dragged down by the weight of substantial debt. Once the hole got to be this size, I could not imagine how I might fill it in, and so I just assumed it would always be there.

Living on Plastic

The only thing remarkable about this story is that, at this point in history, it is completely ordinary. In fact, it is a far happier story than those being lived out by millions of Americans whose phones never seem to stop ringing. With more bills than cash, they have fallen behind and are unable to make even the minimum payments on all their credit card accounts. Collection people from banks and stores call daily demanding payment, and to avoid these embarrassing conversations, many debtors use their answering machines to screen calls. After longer periods of delinquency or nonpayment, the debt is often sold to private collection agencies, whose callers are sometimes aggressive and threatening. Although there are laws against harassment by collection agencies, the laws are difficult to enforce, and as America's indebtedness has risen and the number of debt collection agencies has grown, consumer complaints have skyrocketed. The Federal Trade Commission receives more consumer complaints about debt collection agencies than about any other industry—66,627 complaints in 2005, over five times as many as were received in 1999. Many of these complaints involve debt collection agents who make harassing calls at all hours, misrepresenting the size and nature of the debt. In violation of the law, callers sometimes contact the debtors' relatives, employers, and neighbors and threaten legal action. Bills, often with special yellow or pink envelopes designed to signal an overdue account, arrive daily, and when things get far enough out of control, there are letters from collection agencies and lawyers. After months or years of this kind of stressful existence, bankruptcy begins to look like an attractive way to stop the steady barrage of phone calls and bills.

The numbers tell us we are living in an era when people save very little and borrow a lot. As a result, problems with debt are commonplace. In the United States, the personal savings rate is at its lowest point since the Great Depression, and in 2006 it went into negative territory. Americans now pay out more than they make. A study conducted in 2005 found that among low- and middle-income families who carried credit card balances, the average total credit card debt was $8,650, and according to the Federal Reserve, in 2006 America's total credit card debt topped $900 billion. As a newly single person in 2003, my salary would have been considered better than middle-income, but my total debt of $12,000 was also above average.

Americans are carrying more debt, and it is taking more of their paychecks to do it. [T]he average household debt burden has skyrocketed in recent years, crossing the 100-percent-of-disposable-after-tax-income line in 2000 and rising to above 120 percent in 2005. In other words, the average debt load of an American family, which was a mere 35 percent of after-tax income in 1952, is three and a half times as high in 2005. The average American household owes 20 percent more money than it makes in a year. Much of this debt is secured by the family home or car, but some of it is unsecured commercial credit: Sears, MasterCard, Visa. The recent spike in the debt burden is blamed, in part, on home equity loans taken out during the boom years of rising real estate prices. Many home-owners took advantage of the combination of soaring home prices and low interest rates to "cash out" some of their newly acquired home equity. But debt requires maintenance—regular monthly payments—and this debt maintenance is beginning to put a squeeze on many household budgets. . . .

The proportion of income needed to pay rents and insurance has remained relatively constant, whereas the burdens of mortgage and consumer debt payments have risen sharply.

The combination of high levels of debt, no savings, and a strained household budget is a formula for disaster. Any sizable jolt, such as illness or loss of a job, can sink the ship, and for an increasing number of Americans, there are more than enough jolts to go around. Over the last thirty years, the personal bankruptcy rate has climbed—in good economic times and bad—with most years marking a new record. In 2004, there were approximately 1.6 million personal bankruptcies, but the actual number of bankrupt individuals was even higher. Because approximately one-third of all bankruptcy filings are married couples filing jointly, the number of individuals declaring bankruptcy in 2004 was approximately 2.1 million. Subtracting out those who are under eighteen years old, this number represents a rate of approximately 1 in every 110 adults.

Slipping Through Their Fingers

Why have Americans found themselves in this precarious situation? The United States has the highest gross domestic product of any nation. Compared to many other places in the world, unemployment is low and wages are high. Immigrants from all over the world go to extraordinary lengths—often risking death—to come to this country in pursuit of economic advantage. Although many of the products that symbolize the American way of life are now made in other countries, the United States is the most highly sought-after of all

"Deadbeats" and "Revolvers"

In early 2006, the approximately 190 million bank credit cardholders in the United States possessed an average of about 7 credit cards (4 bank and 3 retail) and they charged an average of $8,500 during the previous year. In 2005, about 75 million (2 out of 5 account holders) were convenience users or what bankers disparagingly refer to as *deadbeats* because they pay off their entire credit card balances each month. In contrast, nearly 3 out of 5 cardholders or over 70 million are lucrative debtors or *revolvers*; they typically pay more than the minimum monthly payment (previously 2% and transitioning to 4% of outstanding balance . . .) while nearly 45 million struggle to send the minimum monthly payment.

Over the last 10 years, 1996–2005, which includes the longest economic expansion in American history, the total number of bank credit cards increased 46.2 percent, total charge volume doubled (from $798.1 to $1,618.0 billion), and "gross" outstanding credit card debt climbed 75 percent. Today, late 2006, approximately three out of five U.S. households account for almost $770 billion in outstanding, "net" bank credit card debt plus over $100 billion in other lines of credit.

Robert D. Manning,
"Prepared Statement of Robert D. Manning, PhD,
Before the U.S. Senate Committee on Banking, Housing,
and Urban Affairs," January 25, 2007.

markets, and American culture is exported throughout the world in television and film images. By any number of measures, we have everything we—and the rest of the world—could possibly want. But for all too many Americans, the good life is slipping through their fingers.

It often seems like we are living in a kind of anxious, foggy dream. Even if our own financial world is stable, on some semiconscious level we have a sense that for many people—perhaps even people we know—something is very wrong. Watching television late at night, after all the commercials for luxury cars and diamond necklaces have slipped away, advertisements appear offering to consolidate your debt into "one easy monthly payment," to "work with your creditors" to reduce your payments, or to arrange for you to get a new credit card "even if you have been denied credit in the past." Advertising on television—even at night—is expensive, so there must be a substantial market for these products aimed at the downtrodden.

For most Americans, it is still taboo to discuss matters of personal finance. Unless things get truly desperate, the details of our neighbors' household balance sheets are hidden from view, and we tend to assume things are going just fine. If our own economic house is in free fall, it is often possible to hide it from others almost indefinitely. Although finding myself $12,000 in the hole in the summer of 2003 was bad enough, it might have been much worse. Over the years, the credit limit on my MasterCard account gradually grew to $25,000. Furthermore, without my asking them to, Sears converted my store charge card into a Sears MasterCard account that, like any MasterCard, can be used wherever the card is accepted. The credit limit on this account was set at $15,000. So without trying very hard, I could have spent another $28,000. It is easy to see how you might go on vacations or buy expensive items that would give your friends the impression you are doing fine, while at the same time, behind closed doors, you are rummaging under the sofa cushions in search of lunch money for the kids.

It helps if you have a good salary. The steady stream of paychecks makes it easier to make regular payments to your creditors. But credit is available to those who want it, whether they have income or not. My students, most of whom are still a few years away from full-time work, are flooded with credit card offers. They receive solicitation calls in their dorm rooms, and tear-off applications for Visa and MasterCard accounts are posted on bulletin boards throughout campus. For those who have both steady income and a good credit record, the solicitations are endless. My mailbox seems to produce an average of one or two credit card offers per day, and I also get them on a regular basis in the mail at work. On television we hear advertising slogans, such as "We're where you want to be," "For everything else there's MasterCard," and "Don't leave home without it." Credit—or, perhaps more accurately, debt— seems to be there for the asking. In the summer of 2003, I had a total of $40,000 available to me on the cards I had in my wallet, but if I had taken on the task of searching for credit and mailed in all the applications I received, there is no telling how much money I might have found. And for people who have lower income than I do, the situation is not much different. If you set out to hang yourself, the banks and credit card companies are more than willing to give you the rope.

An Epidemic of Financial Failure

In 1999, Ed Flynn and Gordon Bermant of the U.S. Department of Justice conducted a study of the demographics of people who declare Chapter 7 bankruptcy, the most common form of bankruptcy under Title 11 of the U.S. Code. They found that the median income of a single woman who filed for bankruptcy was $16,000 per year, which was only slightly below the $17,000 median income for single women in general. The median income for single men in 1999 was $27,000— substantially higher than for women. However, the median income for single men filing for Chapter 7 bankruptcy was approximately $20,000. This amount was also higher than for women, but among those single people desperate enough to declare bankruptcy, the gender gap was greatly reduced. The average income levels of these men and women seeking protection from their creditors were well above the poverty level for 1999, which was set at an annual income of $8,667, but single people declaring bankruptcy tend to reside on the lower half of the income curve. Furthermore, the figures for married people and for larger families are similar. The great majority of bankruptcy cases involve people who are not officially poor but who have less money than most of us. A $20,000 salary provides only $1,700 per month.

The largest single category of debt carried by Americans who pass through the bankruptcy courts is balances on bank credit card accounts, such as Visa, MasterCard, and Discover, but debtors often owe money on store credit cards, utilities, loans, and rent. In relation to the debtor's financial resources, the total burden of debt is often staggering. The average single woman filing for Chapter 7 in 1999 had unsecured debts that were 1.5 times her gross annual income. For men the number was 1.1 times their annual income, but, of course, they made more money, so the average total debt for men and women was roughly equal. Typically, men and women owed approximately $22,000 and $24,000, respectively.

The picture painted by these statistics is quite somber. In 2004, every day the United States bankruptcy courts were open, on average more than six thousand new cases were filed; because many of these involved married couples, a total of at least eight thousand Americans per day declared personal financial failure. As we will see, these figures have come down somewhat since the passage of the bankruptcy bill of 2005, but it is too soon to say how long this decrease will last. Furthermore, although bankruptcies may be down for the moment, every other indicator of financial distress continues to rise unabated. There is little doubt we are experiencing an epidemic of financial failure—an epidemic of enormous dimensions that has gone largely untreated.

| "Many [credit card] consumers . . . don't
have much choice but to scale back."

Credit Card Consumerism Is Ending

Kimberly Palmer

In the following viewpoint, Kimberly Palmer contends that decades of conspicuous and excessive credit card consumption in the United States are coming to an end. Facing high consumer debt, plunging real estate values, and escalating gas and food prices, Americans are cutting back on credit cards, spending less, and saving more. She also predicts that borrowing will be more difficult as interest rates spike. Overall, the financial crisis of 2008 and its call for frugality, Palmer determines, will leave a deep impression on future generations of consumers. Palmer is an associate editor at U.S. News & World Report, *where she also writes a personal finance blog,* Alpha Consumer.

As you read, consider the following questions:

1. As stated by the author, what are emerging as status symbols?

2. What led to the boom in American consumerism, in the author's view?

3. According to Palmer, why do some economists believe Americans will return to conspicuous consumption?

When it comes to longevity, few royals can top America's King Consumer. For more than four decades, our shopaholic nation has shown an insatiable desire to spend until our credit cards melt. And throughout this era, consumer spending has, well, *consumed* a greater and greater share of our total economy. Only twice since 1965, despite half a dozen recessions, have Americans spent less in a year than the previous one. Indeed, it often seems that we have defined ourselves by our ability to buy supersized everything, from McMansions to tricked-out SUVs to 60-inch flat-screen televisions—all enabled by decades of cheap credit.

On the surface, it may seem that there's nothing wrong with all that conspicuous consumption, especially for the biggest, most productive economy on the planet. After all, our undying love of stuff has helped fuel a global economic boom. Yet today, America finds itself at a once-or-twice-a-century economic tipping point. A sharp slowdown, record-high gas prices, high consumer debt levels, a plunging real estate market, and the growing green movement all seem to be conspiring to dethrone King Consumer and transform the economy and the American way of life for years to come. "The process of bringing our wants and our needs into realignment," says Merrill Lynch economist David Rosenberg, "is going to involve years of savings and frugality." Or, to put more it more simply, "there is an anti-bling thing going on," says Marian Salzman, chief marketing officer of Porter Novelli.

Party's Over

Many consumers, of course, don't have much choice but to scale back. Total credit card debt has increased by over 50 percent since 2000. The average American with a credit file is responsible for $16,635 in debt, excluding mortgages, according to Experian, and the personal savings rate has hovered close to zero for the past several years. High gas and food prices are causing real incomes to fall. Even worse, rising inflation will probably cause the Federal Reserve to start jacking up interest rates once the credit crisis on Wall Street has passed, tightening credit even further. "We're shedding jobs, it's much harder to borrow, and what used to be capital gains are now capital losses," says Scott Hoyt, senior director of consumer economics at Moody's Economy.com. "There's no source of funding for spending." Because many of us won't be able to as easily use our homes as ATMs, Hoyt expects to see an upward trend in saving and slower growth in consumer spending, compared with the binge of the past decade.

It was our appetite for housing, after all, that served as the catalyst for the multidecade consumer boom. Consider this: Consumer spending has risen to just over 70 percent of the U.S. economy from a bit more than 60 percent in 1965. The pace really picked up in the 1970s, when the first baby boomers started buying and furnishing their own homes. But now, Rosenberg says, the median boomer is in his early 50s and looking to unload his fleet of leased SUVs.

To some degree, then, demographics are destiny. Longer term, an aging population will need to spend less and save more for retirement. As that process plays out, consumer spending may become less important in the big economic picture. Moody's Economy.com forecasts that the combination of demographic and financial factors will cause just such a seismic economic shift. Reversing a four-decade ascent, consumer spending could actually start falling as a percentage of U.S. gross domestic product, slipping to 68 percent over the next seven years.

Shopped Out

And this new frugality might actually be OK with many of us. Consumers were "so glutted on everything that they had acquired and all the time that was robbed from them. . .that they almost saw this [downturn] as a great opportunity to stop," says Faith Popcorn, chief executive of her eponymous consultancy. In a recent survey, she found that 90 percent of respondents said they were considering options for "the simpler life," and 84 percent said they were inclined to buy "less stuff."

Another survey found that people rank being in control of their finances and living a green lifestyle higher as signs of success than having money or a luxury car, and view having a paid-off mortgage as more of a status symbol than having a beautiful home. "We have to convince ourselves that the lifestyle we can afford right now is a desirable one," says Holly Heline Jarrell, a global director at the communications firm Manning Selvage & Lee, which sponsored the survey.

Examples of the mind-set shift abound. Large-vehicle sales declined 5.5 percent during the first six months of 2008, while compact-car sales rose 33 percent, according to J.D. Power & Associates. Piaggio, the company that makes Vespas, reports that scooter sales in June [2008] were up 146 percent over a year earlier. Even daily lattes have been cut; in July [2008], Starbucks announced that it was closing 600 stores in response to reduced consumer traffic. The NPD Group has found that the number of meals made at home has been steadily rising since 2001. "We're coming back to the home," says Harry Balzer, vice president of the firm.

For some people, the downscaling has more to do with a changing definition of cool than with budgeting. The summer blockbuster *WALL-E* depicts a future world where spending and waste have spiraled so out of control that Earth becomes a giant landfill. Magazines play up how celebrity moms like Victoria Beckham, aka Posh Spice, and Heidi Klum shop at

Target for their kids. A simplification industry has spawned an annual Buy Nothing Day, books and blogs about not purchasing anything for a year, and *Real Simple* magazine. One recent post on the Consumerist, an irreverent Web site dedicated to standing up to corporations, contemplated the Geo Metro's transformation from "weak to chic." Consumerist's senior editor, Meg Marco, who used to drive the unstylish but fuel-efficient vehicle herself, says, "When gas is over $4 per gallon, I don't think anyone is any less 'cool' simply because they're seen driving a compact car."

Young consumers in their 20s may be most affected by the shift to simplicity. In focus group research for her upcoming book on generation Y, consumer psychologist Kit Yarrow has found growing interest in secondhand stores. Young shoppers tell her that it's a "way to get new stuff without creating stuff," she says. And because consumers often learn their lifetime shopping habits during their developmental years, Mandy Putnam, vice president at TNS RetailForward, says that members of generation Y may be permanently shaped by today's lessons in austerity, much as their great-grandparents were by the Great Depression.

There's also an environmental component, says personal finance guru David Bach. "I just sat at the kitchen table with my 5-year-old son talking about 'reduce, reuse, recycle'—I couldn't have told you that at 5," Bach says. He recently wrote *Go Green, Live Rich*, which focuses on how helping the earth can coincide with smart financial choices, such as avoiding bottled water and starting a vegetable garden.

Russell Simon, a 26-year-old communications manager for Carbonfund.org, a nonprofit, embodies that way of thinking. He furnished his Washington, D.C., apartment with used furniture found on Craigslist, uses a canvas bag to bring home groceries, and gave up his '99 Subaru Impreza Wagon. He fills his time with activities, like swing dance lessons, that don't involve buying things. While he's glad his anticonsumption ways

A Sign of Consumer Responsibility

A sign of consumer responsibility: shoppers didn't spend as much on gifts they couldn't afford during the holidays [in 2008] as in years past. Average borrower debt—the average of all the credit cards someone holds—edged up 1.96 percent, to $5,729 from $5,619 year over year.

Eileen AJ Connelly,
"Credit Card Delinquencies Decline in 4th Quarter,"
Associated Press, March 9, 2009.

have a positive effect on the environment, Simon's motivations are more self-serving. "It's about uncluttering my mind, uncluttering my space, and allowing me to focus on things that matter," he says.

Cindee Mazzanti, a self-employed 57-year-old living in upstate New York, started downsizing in 2001, when the end of the dot-com bubble made her realize the importance of living within one's means. She sold her home and used the equity to pay off her debts and purchase a smaller home without a mortgage. She also traded in her Ford Freestyle SUV for a more thrifty Ford Focus to lower her own fuel costs and help reduce America's demand for foreign oil. Her monthly living expenses shrank from $5,600 to $1,200. Without debt, she says, she feels free.

Refills

Retailers are doing what they can to woo these new, economy-minded consumers. In April, Starbucks began offering new rewards on its stored-value cards, including free refills on hot and iced brewed coffee and complimentary syrup and soy milk. "This was an opportunity. . .to show Starbucks can be a part of people's lives even when budgets are tight," Brad Stevens, vice president of Starbucks's customer relationship management, says.

But what happens when budgets aren't so tight? Plenty of hardheaded economists say we'll go right back to our prodigal ways. Alan Blinder, economics professor at Princeton University and former Federal Reserve vice chairman, thinks that optimism and the drive to spend are hardwired parts of America's cultural DNA. Blinder expects that even baby boomers will continue the spending spree that has defined most of their lives, buying medical care and golf vacations instead of new cars and larger homes.

Economist David Malpass argues that Americans aren't nearly as bad off as the low personal savings rate suggests because that calculation ignores the buildup of net worth. (If you bought a share of XYZ Corp. in January at $100, for instance, and its value doubled by December, the savings rate measure would still value that investment at $100.) Malpass points out that the average household has $573,379 in assets, including the value of retirement plans and the cash value of life insurance, and only $117,951 in liabilities.

Even if Americans do curtail their spendthrift habits, the result would probably be a healthier and more balanced American economy. Next year, the federal budget deficit is projected to reach almost $500 billion for the first time. America couldn't afford such a fiscal shortfall if foreign investors, such as the Chinese, didn't buy our debt—U.S. treasury bonds. If as a nation we bought a bit less and saved a bit more, economists say, the result would be stronger long-term economic growth. And depending on the kindness of strangers to perpetually finance your lavish spending sure seems risky. If the foreign appetite for U.S. dollar assets abated, says T. Rowe Price chief economist Alan Levenson, the dollar would probably weaken further, reducing Americans' standard of living.

Besides, there is more to the economy than just the consumer. The economic boom of the 1990s was led by business investment, especially in technology, aiding a boost in productivity that continues today. While businesses are holding back on investment because of recession fears, they are likely to beef it up after that threat passes, says Robert Brusca, chief economist at Fact and Opinion Economics.

And Uncle Sam may have a role to play as well by investing taxpayers' dollars to upgrade our national infrastructure and advance alternative energy technologies. "We're at a critical moment," says Benjamin Barber, author of *Consumed*. "In two or three years, we might say, 'We had a moment where the banks were broke, credit cards didn't have much credit left, when Americans were beginning to rethink consumerism, when we really could have turned the page,'" Barber says. "Or we might be saying, 'We talked ourselves back into the old fixes,'" such as rebate checks and even telling Americans directly to go out and spend, as President [George W.] Bush did after 9/11.

With baby boomers' habits well ingrained, it may instead be generation X and generation Y who decide to embrace a simpler, less wasteful lifestyle, rebelling against the conspicuous consumption that their parents helped make the American way of life.

Periodical Bibliography

The following articles have been selected to supplement the diverse views presented in this chapter.

| Chris Anderson | "The Simple Choice," *Newsweek International*, November 28, 2005. |

Matt Broach — "Art and Appropriation," *PopMatters*, May 14, 2009.

Krista Conger — "Watch Not, Want Not? Kids' TV Time Tied to Consumerism," *Stanford Report*, April 12, 2006.

Leah Dobkin — "Teach Your Kids to Be Consumer Conscious," *Ode*, April 2008.

Global Agenda — "Why Does Berkeley Have so Many Priuses?" June 16, 2008.

Hillary Mayell — "As Consumerism Spreads, Earth Suffers, Study Says," *National Geographic*, January 12, 2004.

Ann O'Connor — "Waste Not, Want Not: Earth-Friendly Living Starts at Home," *U.S. Catholic*, April 1, 2008.

Kimberly Palmer with Benjamin R. Barber — "Consumer Culture vs. Civic Values," *U.S. News & World Report Online*, August 23, 2007.

Barbara Righton — "Hooked on the Spending High: Compulsive Shopping Is Pushing Millions to the Brink of Financial Ruin," *Maclean's*, November 26, 2007.

Ingrid Stegemoeller — "My Baggage with Reusable Bags," *Tri-City Herald*, May 26, 2009.

Stephen Young — "Mass Individualism? Mass Produced Culture in Western Society," *Socyberty*, February 4, 2008.

Should Consumerism Be Rejected?

Chapter Preface

Started by New York–based arts organization the Immediate
Life in 1996, Reverend Billy and the Church of Life After
Shopping grew from a one-man sidewalk show to a full-
fledged theatrical production featuring a thirty-five-member
choir, seven musicians, and a set list of original songs and
gospel numbers. In its mission statement, Reverend Billy and
the Church of Life After Shopping asserts, "Consumerism is
overwhelming our lives. The corporations want us to have experiences only through their products."[i] Thus, the group
preaches "for local economies and real—not mediated through
products—experience."[ii]

Formerly a playwright, actor Bill Talen plays the titular
role of Reverend Billy. He wields his catchphrase of "Changel-
lujah!" to passersby, has staged sermons in retail stores like
Wal-Mart and Nike, and is banned from coming within 250
yards of every Starbucks in California. "In our services," Talen
says, "the praise is not for Jesus and all things glorious. It's for
neighborhoods and communities. We're taking the transfor-
mational possibility of gospel music and applying it to the everyday, the mundane."[iii] Indeed, Reverend Billy and the Church
of Life After Shopping have taken their act across the nation
and abroad. Reflecting upon the reactions of audiences and
the press, Talen responds, "People look at my act and wonder:
Is it politics? Is it art? Is it religion? We do that on purpose. . . .
If we're doing our job and resisting consumerism, then people
are going to have problems naming what we are."[iv]

Reverend Billy and the Church of Life After Shopping's re-
sounding take-home message is for people to reject consumerism. But offering a point of criticism of the group, sociology
professor Joshua Gamson suggests, "Of course, with funda-
mentalists of all kinds blowing up themselves, us, and each
other, and with the Catholic Church covering up the sexual

abuses of priests, the critique of . . . apostles of capitalism can seem a bit beside the point."[v] In the following chapter, activists, experts, and other commentators present their arguments as to whether consumerism should be opposed or accepted.

i. Revbilly.com (accessed May 2009)
ii. Revbilly.com (accessed May 2009)
iii. *Guardian*, May 20, 2009
iv. *Guardian*, May 20, 2009
v. *American Prospect*, June 30, 2002.

> *"A growing number of us are recognizing that consumerism and its counterpart, materialism, are inherently unsatisfying, and are casting about for alternative value systems."*

Consumerism Should Be Rejected

Wanda Urbanska

In the following viewpoint, Wanda Urbanska claims that lifestyles driven by consumerism—and the materialistic values it imparts—are burdened with mounting levels of stress, exhaustion, detachment, and harm to the environment. She advocates that people simplify their lives and embrace environmental responsibility, conscientious consumption, community engagement, and frugality. This can be achieved by making changes in every area of living, Urbanska states, from going television-free to scrutinizing purchases to downsizing one's home. The author is co-producer/host of Simple Living with Wanda Urbanska, *a public television show, and author of several books including* Moving to a Small Town *and* Nothing's Too Small to Make a Difference.

As you read, consider the following questions:

1. According to the viewpoint, what are "intrinsic" and "extrinsic" values?

2. What suggestions does Urbanska provide to live below one's means?

3. How does the author describe the relationship between clutter and well-being?

For many of us, the idea of simpler living has a lot of appeal. "Stressed," "stretched," "time-starved" and "cluttered" describe the frantic condition of so many lives today. No doubt about it, Americans have grown weary of the work-spend-consume treadmill; and a growing number of us are recognizing that consumerism and its counterpart, materialism, are inherently unsatisfying, and are casting about for alternative value systems.

Tim Kasser, who holds a doctorate in psychology and wrote *The High Price of Materialism*, explains that genuinely happy people express "intrinsic values" through self-exploration and self-acceptance, by maintaining close personal relationships and developing "community feeling." In contrast, those who exhibit "extrinsic values" associated with the pursuit of wealth, status and image tend to display narcissistic behavior, to be less empathetic, have lower self-esteem and have lifestyles that are less eco-friendly. Even at middle school age, materialistically oriented students are "less likely to do relatively simple things (for the environment) like turn off lights when no one is looking," Kasser says, "and less likely to reuse stuff."

So if you want to get on the track toward happiness—while lowering your carbon footprint—all roads lead to simple living. The simplicity table stands on four legs—environmental stewardship, thoughtful consumption, community involvement and financial responsibility—and strengthening one leg bolsters the others. For instance, when you decide to start commuting on the bus, you'll save money, build community and become a better environmental steward, all in one. To get started, here are a few ideas for achieving a simpler lifestyle:

Scaling Back

Try TV-free living. Disconnect and reconnect. This probably sounds strange coming from me, the host of a television series, but I decided to go TV-free. Most evenings, my 11-year-old son and I enjoy a leisurely dinner (outside in good weather), read, garden, play chess and talk.

Frugality factor: In 2005, the average cable bill was $43 per month. In a year, that adds up to $516.

Consider one vehicle. If you own two vehicles, try scaling back to one to save money and decrease carbon emissions. Consider selling or donating your spare and shifting to public transportation, carpooling, biking or walking. An obvious solution is scheduling shared use of the family vehicle. It's not as hard as you may think.

Minneapolis resident Matt Hendricks bikes 25 minutes daily to his job, leaving the family's one (paid-for) vehicle with his wife and their daughter. "It's a commute, workout and some recreation all rolled into one," Hendricks says. "If we had two car payments, we probably could not own our home."

Frugality factor: In 2008, the estimated cost of owning one vehicle, including financing, insurance, maintenance, fuel and tax is more than $8,000 a year—and growing as gas prices continue to rise.

Live below your means. A sure way to weather turbulent times while working to secure your financial future is to live below your means. If you save and stash 10 percent (or more) of every dollar that comes your way, as the years pass, your savings will start to become substantial. If you're game for ratcheting up this savings campaign, try to save 100 percent of a pay raise or bonus. Another ambitious technique, for a couple, is to live on one income and save the other.

Frugality factor: Every tightwad knows that 10 percent of even small amounts quickly adds up to a bundle.

Buy used. Vehicles, clothing, tools and toys—whenever possible, take advantage of tremendous savings by purchasing gently used goods. Even items such as appliances may drop in price enormously once they're taken from the storeroom floor. But be sure to inspect the merchandise thoroughly before you swipe your card or count your bills, as most used items are sold "as is." Also, consider swapping items or re-purposing what you have. I transformed my mother's favorite 1960s novelty skirt into kitchen curtains, which are full of personality and flair.

Frugality factor: You can save up to 100 percent when you swap or buy used. Some people will even give you things for the effort of carting them off. For free things, check out www.freecycle.org.

Choose local food. Whenever possible, buy locally grown food rather than trucked-in, long-distance food. Shop at farmers markets; buy a share in a CSA (community supported agriculture); and consider planting a garden of your own. Even if you live in an apartment, you can make a container garden by setting out a few pots of peppers or cherry tomatoes on your patio or deck.

Frugality factor: Especially with food prices rising, you can save money by feeding your family in-season organic produce, especially if it's from your garden. And you can't put a price tag on the pride of ownership!

Creating Community

Create community. The decline of community life and personal bonds is one of the worst changes of the last 20 years. According to one recent study, fully one-quarter of Americans have no one in whom they can confide, more than double the number who responded similarly in 1985. Cecile Andrews, author of *Slow Is Beautiful: New Visions of Community, Leisure and Joie de Vivre*, counters this trend with a "stop and chat" program in her Seattle neighborhood. To build bonds with others, Cecile and her husband Paul consciously make small talk with neighbors and try to engage with newcomers. "When you speak to a stranger, you learn to care for the 'other,' a step toward caring for something greater than yourself," she says.

Frugality factor: Building community boosts your health by providing vital human connections that research shows are central to our well-being. Good health saves money. What's more, human connections may pay off in unexpected ways. For instance, by engaging in community life, you may bump into a realtor who passes along a tip about a desirable property.

Build local economies. One of the most crucial things you can do to build community bonds while strengthening your local infrastructure is to vote with your dollars by buying local, even though sometimes you may pay more. "The most important set of things we can do right now is to re-localize our economies in profound ways," says author and climate change activist Bill McKibben. Shopping locally also fosters relationships with merchants, which will benefit you in the long-run.

Frugality factor: Short-term, the payoff of local trade may be hard to see. But you'll help keep companies in business, keeping your economy—and thus your community—on its feet.

Keep a journal. Active reflection is what the soul needs to stay in shape. Journal writing is a way of keeping in touch with yourself. It provides an active forum for contemplation and a written record for future recollection of where your soul has been. Reading past entries helps you trace your journey, recall your former self, and reflect on the future.

A Bigger Part of the Consumer Value Equation

People still want nicer and bigger material things, but once material advancement can be (more or less) taken for granted, other values take on new priority—individual improvement, personal freedom, empowerment, the environment and, in particular, intangibles like experiences, design, spirituality, relationships, self-expression and, of course, happiness. As these values have become a bigger part of life in markets around the world, intangibles have become a more important part of the consumer value equation.

J. Walker Smith, "Happiness Is Looking Up,"
MediaPostBlogs, March 2, 2009.

Frugality factor: It's the cheapest form of therapy. The only cost is your time and the price of a notebook and pen.

Reconnecting to Nature

Reconnect to nature. In our busy, wired lives, it can be all too easy to lose touch with nature—the grandeur of the outdoors that can uplift and soothe us, and helps promote physical and emotional health. Nature provides refuge and offers us a feeling of freedom, fantasy and sanctuary. Richard Louv, author of *Last Child in the Woods: Saving Our Children from Nature-Deficit Disorder*, makes the case that not just children need an active connection to nature, a sense of play and physicality in the outdoors, in order to be attuned to their humanity. "Even as we grow more separate from nature," Louv writes, "we continue to separate from one another physically." A business leader I know in Greensboro, N.C., makes Friday his outdoor day by walking to work and even holding his business meetings while walking with colleagues.

Frugality factor: The good news about the outdoors is that it's still legal, and free, to exercise, garden, picnic and bird-watch outdoors. Don't consider this wasted time; it may be the most valuable thing you do in a day.

De-clutter. Today we live with an unprecedented number of possessions—so many things that they're overwhelming our drawers and closets and migrating into storage spaces. But experts warn that there's a strong connection between physical clutter and mental clutter. "For most people, the more clutter you have, the more depressed you're likely to feel," says Cindy Glovinsky, certified psychotherapist and author of *Making Peace with the Things in Your Life*. But de-cluttering is easier said than done. To prevent getting overwhelmed, try to de-clutter a small space every day, even just a countertop.

Once you get a handle on your clutter, adopt a new habit: scrutinize every item you bring into your home. And when you bring in something new, try to donate or re-purpose something old.

Frugality factor: De-cluttering is absolutely free. And you may unearth some treasures that you can sell for hard cash, or swap for something you do need. Check out www.freecycle.org or www.itex.com to get started in the world of swapping and bartering. You can also create your own barter arrangement locally by simply asking around. I asked the local music store about used pianos, and ended up connecting with a man who lives two doors down from me and no longer had room for his piano.

Choose not-so-big homes. Next time you move, consider downsizing into what noted architect and author Sarah Susanka calls a "not-so-big" house. The trend in new home construction over the past several decades has been larger living spaces accommodating smaller families. Heating, cooling and furnishing these McMansions increases your costs and carbon footprint. My friend Carol Holst, co-director of the national nonprofit Simple Living America, lives happily in a studio apartment in Glendale, Calif. "I live with the greatest richness because I'm not bogged down by cleaning, dusting and caring for things," she says.

Frugality factor: Money savings here is a no-brainer. With a smaller space to heat, cool, furnish and clean, you free up significant resources for other aspects of your life.

As you move in the direction of simple living, don't expect change to happen overnight. Instead, focus on one arena of lifestyle simplification and work on that first. You might decide to devote the summer to transform your family's food choices. Stay with this and get comfortable before moving on to the next category. And if you slip up or backtrack, treat yourself as gently as the kindest teacher would a young student.

"I'm by no means convinced that consumerism and inequality are the worst things in the world, or that we are hurtling towards environmental doom."

Rejecting Consumerism Is Unrealistic

Reihan Salam

In the following viewpoint, Reihan Salam contends that current movements against consumerism, such as "voluntary simplicity" and Dumpster-diving, merely recycle the failed idealism of the hippie generation of the 1970s. In fact, the author argues that yesteryear's bohemians and libertines have reemerged as today's counterculture-savvy capitalists that push self-righteous and expensive green lifestyles. And detractors who have not abandoned the consumer lifestyle, Salam continues, idly expect the government to solve social and economic issues. Salam is associate editor at Atlantic *and a fellow at New America Foundation, a public policy think tank in Washington, D.C.*

As you read, consider the following questions:

1. How does the author describe hippies?

2. According to Salam, what is the "dropout economy"?

3. What is Salam's opinion on tax hikes for the wealthy?

In late May [2008], *New York* magazine noted a highly unusual advertisement that appeared on Craigslist. A young Brooklyn couple had decided to sell virtually everything they owned, from electronics to furniture to designer shoes, for $8,500. As it turns out, the couple was planning on taking their two young children and setting out for the open road. Two weeks earlier, *The New York Times* profiled several other couples who had made a similar choice—to surrender their accumulated possessions and, with toddlers in tow, to leave a dreary, consumption-driven urban existence behind for something nobler and more environmentally sound. One couple, the Harrises, have been chronicling their adventures on a Web site called Cage Free Family, a clever reference to the cage-free hens so dearly loved by the ecologically correct. Though Jeff Harris had achieved financial success as a computer network engineer, he and his wife felt very keenly that they needed to reconnect with the land. And so the Harrises intend to leave bustling Austin, Texas, for the greener pastures, literally and figuratively, of Vermont.

A New Hippie Movement

Now, it could be that these back-to-the-land bohemians are mere curiosities, puffed up by *New York* and *The Times* simultaneously to delight and guilt-trip their status-obsessed readership. No one knows how many Americans are embracing 'voluntary simplicity', whether by becoming 'freegans'—that is, people who dive into rubbish bins for food out of choice, not necessity—or by abandoning suburban ranch houses to live in communes or campers. But my hunch is that these cage-free families represent the coming of a new hippie moment.

The hippies are now remembered mostly as foul-smelling, tie-dye-clad libertines who, when not covered in a thick haze

By permission Adrian Raeside and Creators Syndicate, Inc.

of marijuana smoke or indulging in 'free love', could be found protesting against the Vietnam War or some other supposed outrage perpetrated by 'AmeriKKKa'. At the same time, the hippies represented a very American rebellion against the cultural conformity and political stupor of the 1950s. As the prime beneficiaries of postwar prosperity, the hippies briefly became the first 'postmaterialist' generation. After all, it was, and is, easy to be post-materialist when all your needs are cared for by doting parents. So began a series of occasionally bold, at times ingenious, and often imbecilic 'experiments in living', ranging from the proliferation of middle-American ashrams to anti-authoritarian homeschooling, a cause later embraced by socially conservative evangelicals. The downside of all this is by now very familiar. Licence led, inevitably, to licentiousness. The patriarchy the hippies so bitterly opposed had the advantage of providing children with reliable material support, something children of the Me Generation couldn't always count on.

And yet a great deal of good came out of this fertile moment. America's technological leadership is arguably rooted in the tinkering of young techno-bohemians like Steve Wozniak and Steve Jobs and software visionary Richard Stallman, who fiddled with computers out of utopian enthusiasm. As the left-wing cultural critic Thomas Frank argued in *The Conquest of Cool*, Madison Avenue eventually cracked this countercultural code. The hippie quest for freedom was co-opted by the capitalists. Consider the advertisements that, during the age of cheap petrol, showed hulking SUVs breezily wending their way through exotic landscapes, this despite the fact that in real life these monstrosities would inch along congested roads from subdivision to office park to supermarket and back again in a hellish loop of suburban torment.

The hippies thus traded in their shapeless garb for power suits, eventually giving rise to the corporate-cultural elite we now know and loathe—a group that manages to combine the self-righteousness and self-regard of the hippies with the shallow consumerism that made the 1950s such a drag, man. Lately we've seen the evolution of environmentalism, the hippie cause par excellence, into a consumerist caricature. Earlier this month [June 2008] the Discovery Channel launched Planet Green, a new cable channel dedicated to the green lifestyles of the rich and the vacuous. Suffice to say, the channel's agenda isn't to encourage less consumption so much as more expensive green consumption. It is apposite that the Prius is the ultimate badge of a green sensibility—manufacturing its nickel battery is extraordinarily carbon intense, and buying an ancient Toyota is at least as good for the environment.

The Dropout Economy

There are, however, countervailing trends. Etsy, a much-buzzed-about Internet retailer based in bohemian Brooklyn, directly connects consumers to creators of handmade goods. The goal, for founder Rob Kalin, is to spark a revival in the handicraft sector, and over the long term to build a new, more ecologically sustainable global economy. Granted, this is all slightly ridiculous. You can't build a flourishing economy on knitwear, eccentric earrings, and homemade pashminas alone. But Kalin has tapped into the power of what you might call the dropout economy—the millions of bright women and men who are turning away from soul-deadening office work, and who are also turning away from what the left-wing Cornell economist Robert H. Frank has referred to as 'the positional arms race'. The Harrises and Kalin are, in this sense, opposite sides of the same coin.

Indeed, one can't help but admire the Harrises, and other families who've chosen to 'downshift' their consumption, for putting their money where their mouth is. Whereas others on the liberal Left rue consumerism and inequality, they almost invariably expect the government to step in and solve the problem by, for example, hiking taxes on the rich. You'd think we were children who couldn't help but work longer hours or buy expensive new automobiles in lieu of darning socks and eating thin gruel. What if the real inequality problem isn't a technical problem? What if it really is a moral problem? Not moral as in 'envy is a corrosive thing, so get over it'. Moral as in no tax hike will prevent people from building overlarge houses or custom cabinets at the expense of spending time with family and friends. A culture that is plagued by materialist excess won't be cured by taxes. It can only be cured, if at all, through a revival of postmaterialist values—that is, a revival of hippie values. Assuming Barack Obama [presidential candidate at the time] is elected and he doesn't achieve paradise on Earth by 2012, it is easy to imagine a new generation growing cynical about politics and, like the hippies, deciding to beat the system in their own idiosyncratic ways.

I'm by no means convinced that consumerism and inequality are the worst things in the world, or that we are hurtling towards environmental doom. But wouldn't it be nice if all those who believed these things to be true moved to bucolic communes where they'd busy themselves with handicrafts instead of tormenting the rest of us?

> *"For freegans, the imperative toward owning inanimate objects and purchasing ancillary services only feeds the beast of capitalist economics."*

Freeganism Addresses the Problems of Consumerism

Sergio Burns

The following viewpoint addresses the rise of "freeganism" (a combination of "free" and "vegan") as a way to combat our consumerist-driven society. Sergio Burns explains that freegans combat capitalist society by minimizing waste and reducing pollution. Through hitchhiking, walking, and skating, freegans reduce the pollutions emitted and recycle discarded materials, such as food and other necessities, through a practice of Dumpster diving. Sergio Burns is contributor to Contemporary Arts, Extra, *and* The New Entertainer *as well as the author of the short story collection* Dark Ghosts Rising.

As you read, consider the following questions:

1. According to the viewpoint, what types of people participate in freeganism?

Sergio Burns, "A Freegan World," *In These Times*, September 7, 2007. Reproduced by permission of the publsiher, www.inthesetimes.com.

2. According to the article, how many tons of edible produce does the United Kingdom discard every year?

3. As described in this viewpoint, how do freegans view housing?

Let's imagine the world as a bizarre neighborhood. On the sunny side of the street some individuals are so rich they can afford to live in castles or mansions. They can travel around the globe in hours instead of weeks, and they throw away enough food to feed a small country. The United States alone produces enough to feed the whole world several times over.

Simultaneously, on the darker side of the 'hood, people die unnecessarily of easily remedied ailments and/or lack of food. Every night, millions go to bed starving, our city streets are barracks to armies of the homeless, and the planet we depend on for our existence is being poisoned to death by carbon emissions and industrial pollution.

The Growth of Freeganism

Not willing to accept that the world has to be polarized between the haves and have-nots, a new sect of activists calling themselves freegans (a contraction of the words "free" and "vegan") have set out to change the way we think and act. There are around 400 to 500 freegans in New York City alone, and growing communities of like-minded individuals across the Western world who are living outside of and challenging the established social order.

"I grew up in Australia," says Martin Filla, a 36-year-old freegan now living in London. "A lot of what I saw didn't make any sense to me. I didn't see people sitting down and really sharing meaningfully with each other. They chose to spend more and more time working in jobs they didn't enjoy. I also noticed that the material possessions people had, did not bring true peace and happiness."

Often condemned as "weirdos" or "nuts," in much the same way as members of the now-respectable green movement were referred to in the past, freegans are convinced that a better, more spiritual and humane way of life is possible. Superficially, freeganism may seem like a new age, hippy-dippy approach to the complex machinations of capitalism and an angst-ridden world. And yes, it is perhaps naïve; a utopian view of human potential in a world divided by politics, nationalism and religion. But many freegans are well-educated, articulate people who were once high-flying achievers—smart, go-getting individuals who just happen to reject societal norms.

Alf Montagu, 31, from Sevenoaks, Kent, England has a degree in experimental psychology from Oxford University and he had a well-paid job in marketing when he became "disenchanted" with his lifestyle about 8 years ago. Now he travels the country in a camper van spreading the freegan message. "I thought to myself, 'What have I been educated for? To manipulate people for my own selfish ends?'" he says. "So I gave up my possessions, my flat, my whole way of life. I was letting go of one form of certainty, which was essentially material, and replacing it with a more spiritual certainty, which was more dependent on doing the right thing. I realized I wasn't put on this world to simply work for money."

Madeline Nelson, 51, a former high-ranking employee of a major publishing firm, once spent her weeks jetting between New York and Paris, but she gave up her corporate life and all its luxuries to become a freegan. She belongs to a New York–based group of freegans that formed three years ago from the Wetlands Activism Collective, a group that fights for Earth, human and animal liberation.

"I used to have someone clean my apartment, I bought convenience foods, I went for weekly massages to relieve stress. I shopped for fairly expensive goods—shoes, handbags—just for entertainment," says Madeline. "Now I realize these goods are not rewards at all, that I was selling my time to buy goods I didn't really need and would never satisfy me. I am much happier living with less stuff, more free time to do what I think is right for me and the world, and with closer, more honest relations with friends and family."

Madeline now resides in a working-class district of Brooklyn.

"Desperate times call for desperate measures," she says. "A number of us now feel we're already in those desperate times—that the consequences of environmental destruction caused by global capitalism, and the binge-and-purge consumption pattern it depends on for growth of 'shareholder value' could well be irreversible and could ultimately end, not just the comfortable life as we know it, but life on this planet."

Defining Freeganism

Freegans believe that most of us are complicit in the suffering of our fellow humans and animals, as well as the environmental destruction of the Earth—even those who appear to be fighting for justice. If you buy into the freegan world-view, well-heeled, astronomically rich icons like U2 front man Bono and former Boomtown Rat/Live Aid organizer Bob Geldof can do nothing to halt this rapidly deteriorating situation because they both operate within the very system that is preventing the hungry from being fed and the homeless from finding shelter.

For freegans, the imperative toward owning inanimate objects and purchasing ancillary services only feeds the beast of capitalist economics. They believe that housing is a right not a privilege, so instead of paying rents or mortgages, freegans tend to squat in abandoned buildings or live with groups of friends. Because of the pollution emitted from cars and other fuel-powered modes of transportation freegans prefer to skate, hitchhike, walk or cycle. Most famously—or infamously—freegans advocate minimizing waste by recycling discarded materials, including food, through a practice known as Dumpster diving or, more euphemistically, urban foraging.

"Most of the food we find through scavenging is in packages, in durable plastic bags," Alf says, sounding defensive. "Most of our bin-raiding is done as and when we have the need, usually en route to other things. It is not usually maggot-infested crap you scrape out of a horrible, dirty bin, but usually perfectly good food. Essentially it is quality wealth that is being discarded. Some people are extremely friendly and actively encourage people to come and take food away. Often these are people who can see the common sense in it. At the other extreme there are people who are anxious that people are made aware of how much food is being thrown out."

From thrusting young bucks, eating out at the most fashionable and expensive restaurants that London, Paris and New York have to offer, to raking around dumpsters and garbage piles for food seems a light year of change. It brings to mind a line from a great song "Walking Down Madison" by Kirsty MacColl and Johnny Marr, "From the sharks in the penthouse/To the rats in the basement/It's not that far." Or was it, "From the rats in the penthouse/To the sharks in the basement/It's not that far"? Of course, Alf, Madeline and Martin gave up affluent lifestyles as opposed to losing them.

Fighting Consumerism and Capitalism

According to Alf, some 35 percent of all food in the United Kingdom goes to waste. How many of the estimated 200 million children who go to bed each night starving would that help feed? He also says that according to official figures, the United Kingdom discards 3.3 million tons of perfectly edible produce each year. Alf thinks, however, that this is a gross underestimate. Some foodstuffs, he says, last for weeks and even months after the use-by date has expired.

Who Dumpster-Dives?

Not everyone who Dumpster-dives is homeless or a political radical—or a frat boy preparing for a hazing ritual.

Melissa is a 36-year-old woman who lives in a nice neighborhood near Kingwood [Texas], but she still has a penchant for digging though other people's trash. . . .

"Over the years I've found all kinds of neat stuff on trash piles or in Dumpsters."

Melissa has always been eco-friendly, but Dumpster-diving became a necessity for her when she lost her first husband.

"I was a single mom," she says. "My husband had died when my daughter was young, so we didn't have the money to go to the furniture store and buy new furniture when we needed to. We made do with what we could find."

Unlike hard-core freegans, she has never recovered food from a Dumpster.

"If I got to the point where I couldn't afford food, I'm sure I would, but I've never been to that point."

Now she's doing better financially—her new husband is an engineer for an oil company—but she still forages when she gets the chance.

Keith Plocek, "Free Lunch," Houston Press, *November 5, 2004. www.houstonpress.com.*

Alf describes the freegan movement as a loose coalition of people with a real sense of global injustice. They are delightful souls for sure, and, yes, they do have solid principles.

And they are out there, spreading their message that the world no longer has to accept the plunder of global capitalism. Alf and Martin give talks to university students and hand out freegan leaflets on the street.

Yet, whichever way you look at it, captalism provides freegans with the food they eat, waste or not. So, aren't freegans depending on the system they want to change for their own sustenance?

"I think this is an interesting question, and it's been argued that freegans actually live off capitalism," says Alfred. "But it's about waste. There are enough resources in the world to share with everyone. People shared long before capitalism. It's all about learning to live off less; appreciate what you have and sharing what you don't need. People have been encouraged through capitalism to fight each other for the world's resources."

Maybe he has a point. Doesn't existence involve a pattern of stark and crazy contradictions? On this corner of the neighborhood, greed plunders the planet, damages the lives of individuals and animals, and calls it globalization. In this weird and distorted district, morbid obesity waddles around with tottering famine, ostentatious overspending sleeps with wretched poverty, mansions with unused rooms mock those sleeping on the street.

The freegans have chosen a fight that will be long and difficult. No doubt, these friendly, principled souls who endeavor to change the world have morality on their side. But is it enough?

| *"That's the problem with freeganism—it is hard work."*

Moderate Consumerism Is More Practical than Freeganism

Raina Kelley

Freeganism ("free" and "vegan") is a boycott of capitalism and the alleged harms of consumerism by abstaining from shopping, preventing waste by reclaiming what others discard, and recycling and reusing. In the following viewpoint, Raina Kelley states that her month-long experiment with freeganism turned her into a more conscientious shopper, but that the practice may not be possible for most people. She declares that going freegan complicated, rather than simplified her life, and that the added chores and obligations interfered with her work and relationships. Moderate consumerism, Kelley determines, is a more realistic option. The author is a writer for Newsweek.

As you read, consider the following questions:

1. What is the author's view of consumption in the United States?

2. What did the author report seeing in the garbage?

3. As stated by Kelley, how did being freegan affect her social life?

Before June of this year [2007], I thought only the sad and desperate ate garbage. Then I discovered the freegans. For those new to the term (free + vegan), a freegan is a person who has decided to boycott capitalist society by severely curtailing consumption of resources through reusing, recycling and Dumpster diving. Taking the expression "Waste not, want not" to its extreme conclusion, freegans try not to purchase anything up to and including food. Instead, they rely on bartering and what the rest of us leave for the garbageman. Now a presence in most American cities, freeganism first popped up out West in Seattle and Portland in the mid-1990s. At first blush, freegans might seem odd and peripheral. But I began to wonder: are they a fringe group reminiscent of our primitive past or are they our carbon-neutral future? At a time when the environmental movement is gaining mainstream acceptance, the freegans are actually living the most hard-core beliefs about consumption and sustainability.

America's overconsumption is legendary. We struggle with morbid obesity, use 25 percent of the world's oil and buy houses we can't afford. If the mildest projections are true, we are recklessly contributing to the warming of the planet. OK, we've made some changes, but does anyone really believe that "carbon offsetting" is anything other than eating your cake and having it, too?

Thus an innocent idea was born. I would live as a freegan for a month. I had nine rules: I would be a vegan who bought nothing but local and/or organic food. I would use only ecofriendly transportation, cut my electricity bill in half and erase my carbon footprint. My mantra would be "Recycle, reuse, renew," while never forgetting to reflect on my impact on the Earth before acting. Any money I saved would go into a "Free-

A Fringe Lifestyle

Freeganism is still a small movement not making a huge impact on how "consumerist America" is run. However, this fringe lifestyle reveals that one can live relatively comfortably without a job, a car or even a home—all while living on the excess waste of America's national blessings.

Robert W. Park, "The Great 'Poverty Line' Lie!"
Real Truth, March 18, 2008.

dom Savings Account" and be used toward allowing me to quit my 9-to-5 as soon as possible. That's tough work for an eBay-loving, omnivorous, cigarette-smoking shopaholic. But I was determined to change my profligate ways. I would transform myself into an eco-princess—a green goddess.

That's not exactly what happened. Here is a summary diary of what did.

DAY 1: I want a Diet Coke. I am craving sugar. Sometimes a 75-cent packet of Skittles is all that prevents a co-worker from getting slapped. I haven't been the same since I pitched this story. I see waste everywhere. I feel guilty about everything—doing my laundry, spending a day at the mall, leaving my computer on at night, relaxing in the shower, BUYING FOOD AT THE GROCERY STORE. How can absolutely everything I've been taught to do to survive be wrong?

DAY 2: Caught in the rain, unable to buy an umbrella and late for work is not a good start to this experiment. Luckily, I don't give up in the face of hardship, I whine. Lesson #1: People don't want to hear about your moral superiority or the difficulty of a choice you made voluntarily. It's a bit like models saying their jobs are hard or movie stars complaining about the paparazzi (a bit, just a bit). The only possible response from people is Shut Up! So I did. Briefly.

DAY 3: I watched a freegan "trash tour" (also known as Dumpster diving). Yes, it sounds disgusting, and is illegal in many cities, which is why our lawyers would not let me partake. But you would be surprised at what freegans find in the garbage. I'd bet that you would eat it. I saw trash bags full of bagels so fresh that when they were opened, the air filled with the aroma of freshly baked bread. I also saw canned goods and even toilet paper among the rubbish. The USDA estimates that more than 90 billion pounds of food is wasted in America every year—much of it from inefficient ordering and inventory systems. Combine that with a scarcity of space on store shelves, and grocers cannot afford to let products languish unsold. I also discovered America's Second Harvest. This nonprofit group takes surplus and distressed food and other groceries, distributes it through its network of food banks and thus feeds more than 25 million hungry people a year. So maybe the Freegans have a point.

DAYS 4–6: Who knew you could gather wild parsnips, bay leaves and sorrel for your dinner in Brooklyn's Prospect Park? Freegans think of themselves as urban foragers—they root around in public parks for food. It's fun, but don't mushroom-hunt if you, like me, don't know what you're doing—someone could die.

DAY 8: Who has time to forage after a hard day's work? Why do I have to make all the sacrifices for this planet? Don't let anyone tell you going green is easy. It's not. It's time-consuming, confusing and infuriating. I was doing fine, living my little piece of the American Dream, and now the inconvenient truth is that I feel bad about it. I like the convenience of modern life. That's the problem with freeganism—it is hard work. Under normal circumstances, I constantly run late. But as a freegan, I was late for 83 percent of my obligations—up sharply from 47 percent the previous month. There are just so many things to do—pack my organic lunch, unplug all my chargers, turn off my computer and put scraps in the compost.

DAY 14: I hate being a vegan. I have wide flat teeth in the back for grain and pointy ones in the front for meat—animals are a natural part of my diet. I feel like I'm starving to death out of guilt over being at the top of the food chain. Sure, I've lost 12 pounds and have lots of energy. So what? There had to be some kind of upside to subsisting on Kashi cereal and peanut butter and jelly, I'm craving sushi so badly, I might go and catch my own. Oh, and it is impossible to compost in a house with three cats.

DAYS 24–26: I'm whipsawing wildly from self-righteousness to despair. My poor husband was nearly strangled when he put a non-organic lemon in my iced tea. We are getting a little testy with each other—squabbling over stupid stuff like who gets to press FAST FORWARD on the digital video recorder. Some people say meat makes you aggressive. But meat's got nothing on deprivation. As it turns out, being a freegan is a lonely existence. I didn't want to hang out with my freegan mentors because I feel like a pretender. And I don't want to see my friends. I don't want to be a mooch or a killjoy. That's just what happens when you think most people in the world are living their lives the wrong way.

DAY 31: I expected to go flying back into the arms of my local Target without a glance back. I can't. I would just feel too guilty. And not that free-form kind of liberal guilt because life is harder on some people than it is on me, but real guilt. I know, I whined a lot. It's not easy to make all your decisions in line with your conscience. But we can't deny that our planet is warming and therefore I am hedging my bets. I think I'll try moderation. I've already learned how to turn the lights out when I leave the room. And you know what? I am determined to limit my buying. So one pair of fall shoes won't break my budget or make me feel guilty but 12 pairs would—a distinction that I would not have been able to make four weeks ago. There's too much waste, and I'd like to be part of the solution rather than part of the problem. And with the twelve hundred dollars I saved, I can now retire two weeks earlier than I planned. I'm a changed woman. Recycle, reuse, renew? You bet. Shopping in the trash? Sorry, can't do it.

> *"Taking care not to adopt a state of thought that becomes easily dissatisfied denies the materialistic marketing mentality any power."*

Consumerism Conflicts with Christianity

The Christian Science Monitor

In the following viewpoint, The Christian Science Monitor *argues that by living in a consumerist society, people often find it difficult to separate their religious lives from the materialistic. The article claims that God satisfies every aspect of life and one needs nothing more, therefore defying consumer-driven culture. The viewpoint asks for society to realize that true satisfaction lies in the spiritual realm.* The Christian Science Monitor *is an international news organization that covers news from around the world.*

As you read, consider the following questions:

1. According to the viewpoint, how does Jesus's message change the consumer questions stated at the beginning of the article?

2. As stated in the article, what benefit does putting "Spirit at the core of life" bring?

3. Where does true satisfaction lie, according to the article?

Living in a consumerist culture means being marketed to, paraded with brands, encouraged to buy and buy again, and educated to think that people are defined by the products they purchase. Some would say this is the ultimate economic model. And, yes, one indication of a healthy economy is the exchange of goods and services. But one common model is built on the premise of selling satisfaction and then breeding dissatisfaction—the idea that you want a particular product, and eventually you'll need more. Several questions underlie this marketing model that can influence the consumer. Questions like: How does this product define me? What will it give me? What do I have to do to get it? How long will it last? Can I have it now?

Changing the Consumer Mindset

A recent *Christianity Today* article, "Jesus is not a brand" by Tyler Wigg-Stevenson (January 2009), pointed out that with so many people accustomed to such a consumer mentality, it can be difficult to separate this from our religious lives. He puts forward this sobering observation: "In a marketing culture, the Truth becomes a product. People will encounter it with the same consumerist worldview with which they encounter every other product in the American marketplace."

A closer look at how a consumerist approach applies to our thinking—and impacts our spiritual lives—can be eye-opening, especially when the "product" is our understanding of God or Jesus' teachings.

To truly know the Christ is to understand and selflessly practice the truths Jesus taught. His message, he promised, would satisfy forever. To the woman from Samaria, whom he met at a well, he said: "Everyone who drinks this water will

The Church of Eternal Shopping

Every week we enter the sanctuaries of the Church of Eternal Shopping. Each day we dutifully reflect on media advertising and work diligently so that we can offer our contribution at the cash register. Slogans are the mantras we repeat; products are the manna we seek; and commercials provide values to live by. We are comforted by the marketplace's use of religious language: "We care," "Trust us," "Come Alive!"

Consumerism tells us a story in which we are the main characters, people who live a better life thanks to the products being sold to us. The "golden rule" of these stories is, "You deserve the best and you can buy your way to happiness." And it's attractive to the would-be believers because all it takes to achieve happiness is a trip to the store.

But this religion relies on fear and false hope. Seek out the latest products and you can find acceptance and happiness, but deprive yourself of these products and you may be cast from society, or live a miserable existence. We are swept up in these stories because they make easy sense of the world.

Julie Kincaid, "Chapter 1: The New Religion,"
Overturning the Tables: Consumerism, Children,
and the Church. *Toronto, ON: UCRD, 2008, p. 5.*

get thirsty again. But no one who drinks the water I give will ever be thirsty again. The water I give is like a flowing fountain that gives eternal life" (John 4:13, 14, Contemporary English Version). Jesus's message of truth changes the consumer questions to emphatic statements of truth: I am defined by God. I am satisfied and need nothing to complete my life. I have all that I need right now, and it is forever new and fresh. I am patient and whole. These statements point to one's spiritual identity and defy the materialistic model.

The Message of Satisfaction Through Religion

Perhaps the ultimate "salesman" of Jesus's teachings—someone whose very existence focused on spreading a message—was St. Paul. He put his life in peril, traveled over land and sea, and spoke to people who'd already made up their minds on the subject of their faith, and on their lifestyle choices. Yet, he delivered the same message of health, wholeness, and satisfaction as Jesus did. Paul's message must have been far from a sales pitch. He couldn't just talk about healing. He had to practice it!

At one point—after Paul's message caused an uproar in Ephesus and he traveled to Troas (cities in the Anatolian region of Turkey)—he gave a speech, which the Bible records "continued . . . until midnight." Then, a young man named Eutychus fell asleep in a window as he listened to Paul's long talk. Soon, Eutychus plummeted to the ground and was "taken up dead" (Acts 20:7–12). While the Bible doesn't record Paul's words, it's quite possible he was recounting Jesus's healings, and he must have been explaining the Master's mission and teachings. Now, Paul had to prove it—the Truth that heals—himself. And he did. Eutychus was healed.

Mary Baker Eddy wrote: "The best sermon ever preached is Truth practised and demonstrated by the destruction of sin, sickness, and death. Knowing this and knowing too that one affection would be supreme in us and take the lead in our lives, Jesus said, 'No man can serve two masters'" (*Science and Health with Key to the Scriptures*, p. 201). Putting Spirit at the core of life brings about the healing we yearn for. Taking care not to adopt a state of thought that becomes easily dissatisfied denies the materialistic marketing mentality any power. True satisfaction lies in the understanding that spiritual ideas have such a profound effect on our lives that they lift the lives of others, too, and provide uncountable blessings.

> "In brief, evangelicals are using the market to fashion and refashion themselves, and to project the resulting identity to others, in just the way that all consumers do."

Consumerism Can Benefit Christianity

Jeremy Lott

Many Christians denounce consumerism, particularly when their religious beliefs are commercialized. But in the following viewpoint, Jeremy Lott suggests that consumerism serves the causes of Christianity and its culture. For instance, the growing interest of secular businesses and corporations in catering to Christians is a win against religious intolerance, Lott states. He also adds that the appearance of evangelical books on best-seller lists and Christian artists on pop charts place Christianity into greater view. While the Christian market is not immune to crass commoditization and corporate greed, the author claims that its consumer products allow followers to build a shared identity that is formidable in mainstream culture. Lott is a contributing editor to Books & Culture *and author of* In Defense of Hypocrisy.

Jeremy Lott, "Jesus Sells," *Reason*, February 2003, pp. 41–47. Copyright © 2003 by Reason Foundation, 3415 S. Sepulveda Blvd., Suite 400, Los Angeles, CA 90034, www.reason.com. Reproduced by permission.

As you read, consider the following questions:

1. What Christians' criticisms of the Christian Booksellers Association trade show does Lott provide?

2. How has the economic success of Christian culture affected its original institutions and businesses, in the author's view?

3. According to the author, what is "bibliolatry"?

No doubt the evangelical Christian Booksellers Association (CBA) picked the Anaheim Convention Center for its annual convention last year [in 2002] because the place is enormous and has a certain architectural inspiration. Conventioneers can pause as they approach the huge lobby, with its three-story glass wall, for a view that seems to offer a glimpse of heaven. Unfortunately, Disneyland's Space Mountain ride is always in the way.

When I joined the CBA attendees in Anaheim, row upon row of mostly white men and women dressed in their Sunday best were filing into one of the big conference rooms. CBA President Bill Anderson welcomed us; those present, he said, represented some 50 states and 60 nations. Then he got down to business, as it were.

What followed had all the trappings of a religious service—songs, testimonies, a sermon. Technically, it *was* a religious service. But it was overtly commercialized to a greater extent than any religious gathering I had ever observed (and as the son of a Baptist minister, I've seen a lot of them). The printed programs, for example, were underwritten by the publisher of Pastor Lee Strobel—he'd preached the sermon—and featured an ad for his many books. The singers at the service were in town to promote their latest CDs to retailers.

If the participants felt any shame about the nakedly commercial nature of the event, they did a good job of hiding it. In his invocation prayer, Anderson addressed God on behalf of "a group of colleagues, working together under Your Lordship." Strobel, between jokes and stories about his days as an "atheistic reporter" in Chicago, commended the retailers for doing the Lord's work and assured them that "we've got the truth," thus giving them "an unfair advantage in the marketplace of ideas."

The CBA was nothing if not a marketplace. At 350,000 square feet, the floor of the convention center is nearly the size of eight football fields, including three halls, two outdoor eating areas, and several restaurants. Over the next few days this huge space would be home to almost 500 display booths, over 12,000 people, and even a special Internet café. In its zeal to grow and serve its market, the Christian culture industry mirrors its secular counterpart. As important, it shines a light on how both true believers and non-believers use culture to create all sorts of identities and communities.

Many glass cases displayed such wares as crosses, paintings, color-coded Bibles, T-shirts, mugs, greeting cards, bracelets, CDs, necklaces, children's videos, diet books, jigsaw puzzles, backpacks, board games, and decorative plates. And that was just in the lobby. It wasn't until I got past the security guard, flashing my scarlet-lettered press pass, that I had a chance to see what was on the sales floor.

All of the major evangelical Christian publishers were present in force, with some booths the size of small houses. Older mainstream names such as Doubleday, Penguin, Random House, and Oxford University Press were well represented. Young upstart publishers such as Canon Press and Relevant Books—publisher of such tomes as *Walk On: The Spiritual Journey of U2* and *The Gospel According to Tony Soprano* (do unto others and then split?)—had smaller but still impressive booths. There were several Spanish-language publishers and a couple of African American presses, along with a few Catholic ones. A number of children's publishers sat alongside hawkers of Christian comics. The book area was surrounded by "personality booths," where authors autographed and gave away lots of free books to dealers in the hope of pumping up sales.

Books were only a part of the story. Also pushing their wares were such movie companies as Cloud Ten Productions, music and multimedia booths run by companies such as Word Entertainment, and plenty of Christian "gift" outlets in a section of their own. In addition to the items in the lobby, these gifts included everything from Scripture Mints shaped like little fish ("reaching the world one piece at a time") to hand puppets.

Word Entertainment took the prize for best attention grabber with spotlights, free popcorn, and—I am not making this up—a "Catch the Cash" booth with money swirling around: You stepped into it and grabbed as much as you could as fast as you could. Other memorable promotions included inflatable sharks, Jews for Jesus shopping bags, a guy in a kilt, and one booth that featured a stop sign altered to read, "STOP Liberals!"

The Christian Culture Industry

The CBA may be the only trade show that sets off spasms of conscience among its own participants. Several editors and publishers told me, under condition of anonymity, that they were appalled at some of the products on the floor—and they weren't necessarily sparing their own titles. The Rev. R.C. Sproul Jr., son of a famous Calvinist polemicist, published a brief Internet commentary that considered the possibility of driving out the moneychangers, though he finally concluded that it *is*, after all, a trade show. *Christianity Today* review editor Doug LeBlanc complained to me about the "buffoonery" of such crass gimmicks as the money booth. The promoter with the inflatable sharks sent me a note that made fun of the fish-shaped mints ("Mmmm, minty fresh Scripture").

Nor is this discomfort a new development. In his 1997 book *Mine Eyes Have Seen the Glory: A Journey into the Evangelical Subculture in America*, Columbia University professor of religion Randall Balmer tells of his trip to the 1988 CBA convention. He describes a gathering similar to, if slightly smaller than, the one I attended, including wild promotions, a cornucopia of products, and, of course, fretting by evangelicals over how commercial and gaudy the industry had become. John Pott, an editor at Eerdmans, confessed to finding the whole scene "utterly demoralizing." Publisher Lisa Shaw admitted that she had gotten "so fed up with the whole thing that I went...to my hotel and cried for two hours." If blatant commercialization is cause for tears, it's a wonder that Shaw stopped after only two hours.

The Christian culture industry, as represented both by the CBA convention and by its member stores, may have been less concerned with sales in the past, but I've found little evidence of that. The sense of guilt that hovers over the convention may reflect the growing pains of an industry that is expanding its services to a slice of society whose cultural demands grow each year.

Most Christian book companies started as small family affairs or as publishing arms of Bible colleges; many CBA stores started as mom-and-pop operations. Through a process of sifting, much like what goes on in the secular publishing and bookselling industries, some went bust while others innovated, grew, and sold out to secular publishers who wanted a piece of the Christian action. In fact, most large Christian publishers are now owned by otherwise secular houses. Random House, for instance, owns Zondervan, a leading Christian house. While no Christian chain yet rivals Barnes & Noble, Family Christian Bookstores has several hundred outlets across the country.

The older presses that have not sold out to the secular giants either struggle or get religion, the religion in this case being marketing. One editor of a very conservative holdout told me the only question his publisher asks about a book is whether it will sell. (Theology does play an indirect part in the selection process: If a book's message is likely to offend readers, it probably won't sell.) Publishers that have typically peddled more highbrow fare are experimenting with different sorts of titles. The current catalog of the high-toned house Westminster John Knox Press, for example, features *The Gospel According to the Simpsons*.

In fact, the publisher Thomas Nelson, one of the few holdouts to make it big, recently reversed the familiar process and started a secular imprint, WND Books.

It features such newsmaking authors as former Florida Secretary of State Katherine Harris (now a member of Congress) and shock jock Michael Savage.

Not only is the Christian book industry itself huge, its borders are getting hard to define because so many of its works are published and sold by secular firms. It's difficult to fix the dollar figures with any kind of precision, but sales through CBA member stores and distributors—a large segment but by no means all of the industry—came to $4 billion in 2001.

The best-selling novel that year was not a John Grisham or Tom Clancy number but *The Remnant*, the latest installment of Tim LaHaye and Jerry Jenkins' *Left Behind* series, a feat that landed the authors on the cover of *Time*. As a result, mainstream publisher Bantam Dell signed LaHaye to a reported $45 million book contract for a separate series. Other Christian titles, such as Bruce Wilkinson's *The Prayer of Jabez*, occasionally make ripples in the secular publishing world, and most large bookstores have expanded their sections of religious books and novels. Not long ago, if someone wanted a work by Christian horror writer Frank Peretti or lay theologian Philip Yancey, they would have had to visit a religious specialty store. Now they can find it at Barnes & Noble or Borders.

Evangelical Christian pop music—popularly known as Contemporary Christian Music, or CCM—now rivals country as the most popular radio format. Several acts, from Michael W. Smith to Jars of Clay, have tried "crossing over" to secular markets, with varying degrees of success. New quasi-religious acts like Creed and Litehouse engage in heavy flirtation with the CCM market without explicitly joining it.

Christian filmmaking is also starting to emerge from the swamp of poor distribution and lousy production values. On display at the CBA were such films as *Waterproof* (starring Burt Reynolds), *To End All Wars* (dubbed a film "to end all Christian films" by the religious periodical *Books & Culture*), and *Hometown Legend* (think *Rudy* minus the Hail Marys). The cloth strap that held my convention ID doubled as a promotion for the new *Veggie Tales* movie, *Jonah*, which according to *Box Office Mojo* had taken in over $25 million by Thanksgiving 2002.

Lines of Criticism

Not everybody is happy with the shape and success of the modern Christian culture industry and its growing crossover appeal. In response to the huge LaHaye book deal, critic Bruce Bawer warned on TomPaine.com of the "growing ties between New York publishers and evangelical Christian authors."

Bawer, author of *Stealing Jesus: How Fundamentalism Betrays Christianity* and *A Place at the Table: The Gay Individual in American Society*, expressed nostalgia for an earlier era of publishing when "no reputable New York publisher would have published such books" as the *Left Behind* series in order to get its mitts on vaguely sinister-sounding "evangelical money." "Some of us," explained Bawer, "still cling to the old fashioned idea that the publishing of books in a democratic society, in addition to being a business, is also a profession that carries with it certain moral, intellectual, and aesthetic obligations. . . . The current move into premillenialist prophecy novels and other works of hard core fundamentalism seems a giant step too far."

In case readers missed the other-shoe-dropping implications of his screed, Bawer took a swipe at the patriotism of Bantam Dell and company for "capitulating" to Bible-thumpers "at a time when the United States is waging a war against fundamentalist intolerance and illiberality—against minds and hearts possessed by irrational dreams of violence."

Other lines of criticism come from the constituency of the Christian culture industry itself. To many evangelicals, who after all are Protestants, the gaudy excesses of the industry trigger vague cultural memories of ancient controversies over relics and indulgences. The Reformers viewed the marketing of religious artifacts and get-out-of-purgatory-free passes as a sign of decay. It's a pretty good bet that John Calvin or Martin Luther would be none too thrilled by the Jesus, Mary, and Joseph action figures or the Christian self-help books (as one author put it, "It's like a regular motivational book with Bible verses sprinkled in") displayed on the CBA convention floor.

This queasiness is reinforced by an anti-materialist streak that American evangelicalism seems to have absorbed during the 1960s and '70s. In fact, evangelicals' professed contempt for material things can rival the anti-consumerism of the most ardent Naderite [referring to Ralph Nader]. A popular anti-materialistic evangelical song from the '60s featured the refrain "they'll know that we are Christians by our love." When I suggested to evangelical acquaintances that it's just as likely that "they'll know that we are Christians by our stuff," it produced a lot of exasperated sighing.

Another criticism of the culture industry, expressed from within as well as without, is that it has a tendency to reinforce a certain insularity in evangelicals. In the 1980s evangelical singer-songwriter Steve Taylor mockingly expounded on the benefits of the industry: "You'll be keeping all your money/in the kingdom now/And you'll only drink milk from a Christian cow." In the 1990s a secular narrator of one of the vignettes in Douglas Coupland's novella *Life After God* expressed this distance by reporting on his attempt to understand the "many many" Christian radio stations he happened upon as he drove through a desert. He sensed a real enthusiasm he ultimately failed to penetrate:

> The radio stations all seemed to be talking about Jesus non-stop, and it seemed to be this crazy orgy of projection, with everyone projecting onto Jesus the antidotes to the things that had gone wrong in their own lives. He is Love. He is Forgiveness. He is Compassion. He is a Wise Career Decision. He is a Child Who Loves Me.

Evangelicals in Plain Sight

Critics are right about the apparent insularity of evangelical culture, but not as right as they think they are. The hand wringing that the *Left Behind* series has engendered, for instance, is irrational. Though Bruce Bawer's Tompaine.com piece is an extreme example of overreaction, a few nonreligious friends have privately explained to me that the existence and popularity of such books—"wish fulfillment fantasies about non-fundamentalists suffering apocalyptic torment," as Bawer put it—worry them. The reviewer for the determinedly anti-religious *Free Inquiry* likened the series to *The Turner Diaries*, the anti-Semitic survivalist underground classic that helped inspire Oklahoma City bomber Tim McVeigh.

Yet, other popular novelists, Stephen King among them, are often just as apocalyptic as LaHaye and Jenkins, without inspiring dire warnings that America is about to embrace a fascist theocracy. True, King and company don't take their apocalypses seriously. On the other hand, the end of the world has been a popular subgenre for many years. Exactly what has

Sales of Christian Books Are Increasing

In 2004:

- 7 percent of all books sales were represented by religious titles

- $1.95 billion Net revenues from sales of religious books

- $26.45 billion Net revenues from sales of all books.

Heather Grimshaw, "An Almighty Market God Is Big Business in the Publishing World," The Denver Post, July 10, 2005.

drawn readers to so many secular total destruction fantasies is a question that's hard to answer, but that answer is unlikely to be compassion for humanity.

In any event, one might hazard that the incomprehension of secular outsiders has contributed significantly to the birth of the commercial Christian pop culture scene. That is, while the books, music, and videos in CBA stores may not have been of the highest quality or featured the best production values, they at least took seriously the beliefs held by evangelicals, who may constitute anywhere from a quarter to a third of American society. The move by secular presses, movie studios, radio stations, and record labels to cater to this market could be viewed as a victory for commercial self-interest over religious intolerance.

In fact, the economic embrace of Christian pop culture by mainstream producers may be straining the original Christian cultural scene. Now that evangelical novelists can be published by secular presses, they can avoid relatively stifling moral guidelines that have been constraining them (no swearing, no sex out of marriage unless it has disastrous consequences, the requisite amount of God talk, etc.). New Christian music acts are now routinely courted by secular record labels. That allows them more freedom to inject their faith into the mainstream culture in a way that simply wasn't done by secular labels before, even while removing the more popular groups from the Christian labels' lists. Christian publishers are being squeezed at both ends as bookstores demand steeper discounts while increasingly influential mainstream agents secure better contracts for Christian writers. In turn, Christian bookstores face new competition from secular bookstores.

Sales of Christian books through nonreligious bookstores are also rectifying a long-running, quasi-conspiratorial grievance of many evangelical authors, because it allows their books to climb best-seller lists from *The New York Times* to *USA Today*. Such lists only count sales through mainstream bookstores, which in the past effectively excluded even the most wildly successful evangelical best-sellers from recognition. This division of secular and religious book sales, like the division of secular and religious culture in general, had the effect of removing evangelical culture from the view of those who were not a part of that subculture.

Now that this industry is increasingly in plain sight, its relationship with its consumers can be studied. It turns out that the industry is neither as sinister and monolithic as secular critics claim nor as secular and venal as religious critics fear.

Randall Balmer, the religion professor, describes Christian culture as the product of a separatist impulse that managed to yield results very similar to the secular culture Christians sought to escape. Superficially, he has a point. As I wandered down the aisles of the CBA, I asked the same question: Hasn't the industry simply replaced self-help and pop psychology books with pious variants thereof, the secular *Butt Ugly Martians* with the religious *Veggie Tales*, Altoids with Scripture Mints, Beanie Babies with Holy Bears, and secular schlock apocalyptic novels with tamer, preachier Christian schlock apocalyptic novels? On first blush, it sure looks that way.

But the distinction between the material and the sacred, or the commercial and the spiritual, can be tricky. To pick an obvious example, there is no more sacred book to evangelicals than the Bible—more tradition-minded Christians sometimes accuse them of "bibliolatry," the worship of the text—and there is no product of the Christian culture industry that is more effectively exploited and marketed than the Good Book.

At the convention were dozens of different translations and paraphrases of the Bible—the New International Version, the King James, the New King James, The Message—along with hundreds of specialty Bibles with commentaries (by rock musicians as well as serious Bible scholars), and countless freestanding commentaries on individual biblical books. (The existence of red-lettered editions of the Bible, in which the words attributed to Christ appear in red, serves as the set-up for an awkward situation in Christopher Moore's *Island of the Sequined Love Nun*. The clueless hero asks a Bible-reading guard if the red writing highlights all the juicy parts.)

Or take other, more suspect items from the convention: those Scripture Mints, holy diet books, spiritual key chains, Thomas Kinkade paintings, biblical action figures—all items that your local evangelical bookstore is likely to carry. Surely these items are shameless and naked grabs for evangelical filthy lucre. What possible purpose, skeptics ask, can such kitsch serve?

The Real Significance

Are many of these products merely a way to make a fast and cynical buck? They probably are. But the more revealing question is not about what the products do for their producers; it is about what they may be doing for their consumers.

The anti-materialistic/anti-consumerist criticism overlooks an essential fact: that material artifacts, even kitsch, can embody real meaning for those who use them.

The products, good and bad, that dominated the CBA both reflected and validated the subculture that generated the demand for them. The people who read the books, listen to the music, hang the Thomas Kinkade paintings in their homes, and use the other products of this industry are surrounding themselves with artifacts that reflect their values and beliefs, that validate who they are. For such consumers, the *Left Behind* novels, the evangelical pop music, and all the rest serve as the building blocks of a shared evangelical cultural identity. In brief, evangelicals are using the market to fashion and refashion themselves, and to project the resulting identity to others, in just the way that all consumers do.

Therein lies the real significance of the Christian cultural industry. It is fixed enough to support a religious group identity for millions of people but fluid enough to accommodate myriad arguments and interpretations. And it gives this minority religious group the ability to make the wider culture take it seriously—to punch above its weight in the market contest it has entered.

Periodical Bibliography

The following articles have been selected to supplement the diverse views presented in this chapter.

| Rachel Barnes | "Ethical Shopping: Is It a Meaningless Concept?" *Grocer*, February 9, 2008. |

| Helen Brown | "Froogles: The New Challenge to Rampant Consumerism," *Independent*, October 5, 2006. |

| Jessica Brown | "Riding the Ethical Wave," *Investment Adviser*, January 22, 2007. |

| Sergio Burns | "Freegan World," *In These Times*, September 7, 2007. |

| Edward Comor | "I'm Dreaming of an Orgiastic Christmas," *COA News*, December 11, 2006. |

| Karen Goldberg Goff | "Crafty Comeback with Indie Edge," *The Washington Times*, May 27, 2009. |

| Marta Mae and Sara Victoria | "What Is Ecofashion?" *Habitat Australia*, April 2008. |

| David Smith | "Stop Shopping . . . or the Planet Will Go Pop," *Guardian*, April 8, 2007. |

| Anthony Stevens-Arroyo | "Only Bad Capitalists Go to Heaven," *The Washington Post*, September 19, 2008. |

| Natalie Zmuda | "Is Earth Day the New Christmas?" *Waste News*, April 28, 2008. |

For Further Discussion

Chapter 1

1. Kevin A. Hassett and Aparna Mathur state that consumption is an indicator of economic well-being. Do you agree or disagree with the authors? Use examples from the viewpoints to support your answer.

2. Brendan O'Neill argues that rising rates of psychological disorders can be attributed to the "therapy culture" that pathologizes normal emotions. In your opinion, does Tori DeAngelis participate in therapy culture in her viewpoint? Explain your answer.

3. Do *Knowledge@Wharton* and Joseph Epstein share the same views of luxury? Use examples from the viewpoints to explain your answer.

Chapter 2

1. Anup Shah states that advertising promotes consumerism. On the other hand, Charles Shaw alleges that consumerism can be linked to addictive behavior. In your view, who makes the most compelling argument? Explain your answer.

2. Rick Wolff contends that consumerist values pushed Americans to work harder and overspend, leading to a financial crisis. Do you agree or disagree with Wolff? Use examples from the viewpoints to explain your answer.

3. In your opinion, do Alex Williams and Zachary Karabell share similar or different views of the average middle-class American? Use examples from the viewpoints to explain your answer.

Chapter 3

1. Karen Sternheimer claims that fears about consumerism and children are based on adults' fears and anxieties. In your view, does Kris Berggren's viewpoint rely on these fears and anxieties? Use examples from the viewpoints to support your response.

2. Frank Furedi accuses green consumers of elitism. Do you agree or disagree with the author? Explain your answer.

3. Stuart Vyse draws from personal experience to demonstrate how reliance on credit cards led to debt. In your opinion, did Vyse depend on credit irresponsibly? Explain your answer.

Chapter 4

1. Reihan Salam insists that rejecting consumerism is idealistic. In your opinion, does Wanda Urbanska offer idealistic alternatives to consumerism? Use examples from the viewpoints to support your response.

2. In her viewpoint, Raina Kelley recounts practicing freeganism for a month. In your view, is freeganism a viable alternative to consumerism? Explain your answer.

3. A writer at *The Christian Science Monitor* suggests that Christians should realize that true satisfaction lies in the spiritual realm, not in consumerism. Jeremy Lott claims that many Christians do denounce consumerism. In your opinion, are these authors correct? Why or why not?

Organizations to Contact

The editors have compiled the following list of organizations concerned with the issues debated in this book. The descriptions are derived from materials provided by the organizations. All have publications or information available for interested readers. The list was compiled on the date of publication of the present volume; the information provided here may change. Be aware that many organizations take several weeks or longer to respond to inquiries, so allow as much time as possible.

Cato Institute
1000 Massachusetts Avenue NW
Washington, DC   20001-5403
(202) 842-0200 • fax: (202) 842-3490
Web site: www.cato.org

Founded in 1977, the mission of the Cato Institute is to increase the understanding of public policies based on the principles of limited government, free markets, individual liberty, and peace. The institute aims to use the most effective means to originate, advocate, promote, and disseminate applicable policy proposals that create free, open, and civil societies in the United States and throughout the world.

Consumer Action
221 Main Street, Suite 480, San Francisco, CA   94105
(415) 777-9635
Web site: www.consumer-action.org

Consumer Action is a nonprofit, membership-based organization that was founded in San Francisco in 1971. Consumer Action has continued to serve consumers nationwide by advancing consumer rights; referring consumers to complaint-handling agencies through its free hotline; publishing educational materials in Chinese, English, Korean, Spanish,

Vietnamese, and other languages; advocating for consumers in the media and before lawmakers; and comparing prices on credit cards, bank accounts, and long-distance services.

Consumer Federation of America (CFA)
1620 I Street NW, Suite 200, Washington, DC   20006
(202) 387-6121
e-mail: cfa@consumerfed.org
Web site: www.consumerfed.org

The Consumer Federation of America (CFA) gathers facts, analyzes issues, and disseminates information to the public, policy makers, and the rest of the consumer movement. The size and diversity of its membership—approximately 280 non-profit organizations throughout the nation with a combined membership exceeding 50 million people—enables CFA to speak for virtually all consumers. In particular, CFA advocates for those who have the greatest needs, especially the least affluent.

Consumer Watchdog
1750 Ocean Park Boulevard, Suite 200
Santa Monica, CA   90405
(310) 392-0522 • fax: (310) 392-8874
e-mail: admin@consumerwatchdog.org
Web site: www.consumerwatchdog.org

Consumer Watchdog (formerly the Foundation for Taxpayer and Consumer Rights [FTCR]) is a nationally recognized consumer group that has been fighting corrupt corporations and dishonest politicians since 1985. Over the years, Consumer Watchdog has worked to save Americans billions of dollars and improved countless peoples' lives by speaking out on behalf of patients, ratepayers, and policyholders.

Federal Trade Commission (FTC)
Consumer Response Center, Washington, DC   20580
(877) 382-4357 (FTC-HELP)
Web site: www.ftc.gov

The Federal Trade Commission (FTC) deals with issues that touch the economic life of every American. It is the only federal agency with consumer protection and competition jurisdiction in broad sectors of the economy. The FTC pursues vigorous and effective law enforcement; advances consumers' interests by sharing its expertise with federal and state legislatures and U.S. and international government agencies; develops policy and research tools through hearings, workshops, and conferences; and creates practical and plain-language educational programs for consumers and businesses in a global marketplace with constantly changing technologies.

Free Market Foundation (FMF)

903 East Eighteenth Street, Suite 230, Plano, TX   75074
(972) 423-8889 • fax: (972) 423-8899
e-mail: info@freemarket.org
Web site: www.freemarket.org

The Free Market Foundation (FMF), which was founded in 1972, is a nonprofit organization dedicated to protecting freedoms and strengthening families in Texas and nationwide. It stands for First Amendment freedoms, less government, and solid family values. FMF is one of the few groups in the country that has a legislative and a legal department, Liberty Legal Institute, staffed with full-time attorneys experienced in litigation.

Green America

1612 K Street NW, Suite 600, Washington, DC   20006
(800) 584-7336
Web site: www.coopamerica.org

Green America is a not-for-profit membership organization founded in 1982, going by the name Co-op America until January 1, 2009. Its mission is to harness economic power—the strength of consumers, investors, businesses, and the marketplace—to create a socially just and environmentally sustainable society.

SustainAbility
Washington Office, 1638 R Street NW, Suite 301
Washington, DC   20009
(202) 315-4150
e-mail: washington@sustainability.com
Web site: www.sustainability.com

Established in 1987, SustainAbility advises clients on the risks
and opportunities associated with corporate responsibility and
sustainable development. Working at the interface between
market forces and societal expectations, it seeks solutions to
social and environmental challenges that deliver long-term
value. SustainAbility's research addresses topics as diverse as
the future of globalization, lobbying, governance, supply
chains, and corporate accountability.

Truth About Credit
44 Winter Street, Boston, MA   02108
(617) 747-4330
Web site: http://truthaboutcredit.org

Truth About Credit is a project of the U.S. Public Interest Research Group (PIRG) Education Fund and the Student PIRGs.
U.S. PIRG works to pursue a mission of standing up to powerful interests on behalf of the public. U.S. PIRG conducts research, education, and advocacy on behalf of consumers. With
the help of a professional staff of advocates and organizers,
the Student PIRGs investigate problems and develop practical
solutions and aim to convince the media and decision makers
to pay attention and take action on consumer protection and
higher education issues.

Bibliography of Books

Benjamin
R. Barber

Consumed: How Markets Corrupt Children, Infantilize Adults, and Swallow Citizens Whole. New York: W.W. Norton & Company, 2007.

Arthur Asa Berger

Shop 'Til You Drop. Lanham, MD: Rowman & Littlefield, 2005.

Shira Boss

Green with Envy: Why Keeping Up with the Joneses Is Keeping Us in Debt. New York: Grand Central Publishing, 2006.

Alain de Botton

Status Anxiety. New York: Pantheon Books, 2004.

Robert Frank

Falling Behind: How Rising Inequality Harms the Middle Class. Berkeley: The University of California Press, 2007.

Lilia Goldfarb

"Buying into Sexy": Preteen Girls and Consumerism in the 21st Century. Saarbrücken, Germany: VDM Verlag, 2009.

John Grant

The Green Marketing Manifesto. Hoboken, NJ: Wiley, 2008.

Paul Hawkin,
Amory Lovins,
and L. Hunter
Lovins

Natural Capitalism: Creating the Next Industrial Revolution. New York: Bay Back Books, 2008.

Joseph Heath and
Andrew Potter

Nation of Rebels. New York: Collins Business, 2004.

Jean-Noël Kaperer and Vincent Bastien — *The Luxury Strategy: Break the Rules of Marketing to Build Luxury Brands.* Philadelphia, PA: Kogan Page, 2009.

Annie Leonard — *The Story of Stuff: How Our Problem with Overconsumption Is Trashing the Planet, Our Communities and Our Health—and What to Do About It.* New York: Free Press, 2010.

Martin Lindstrom — *Buyology: Truth and Lies About Why We Buy.* New York: Doubleday, 2004.

Iris Nowell — *Generation Deluxe: Consumerism and Philanthropy of the New Super-Rich.* Ottawa, Canada: Dundurn Press, 2004.

Alissa Quart — *Branded: The Buying and Selling of Teenagers.* New York: Basic Books, 2004.

Al Ries and Laura Ries — *The Origin of Brands: How Product Evolution Creates Endless Possibilities for New Brands.* New York: Collins Business, 2004.

Juliet Schor — *Born to Buy: The Commercialized Child and the New Consumerism.* New York: Simon & Schuster, 2004.

Barry Schwartz — *The Paradox of Choice: Why More Is Less.* New York: HarperCollins, 2004.

Herb Sorensen — *Inside the Mind of the Shopper: The Science of Retailing.* Upper Saddle River, NJ: Wharton School Publishing, 2009.

Thomas Sowell — *Basic Economics: A Common Sense Guide to the Economy*. Cambridge, MA: Basic Books, 2007.

Dana Thomas — *Deluxe: How Luxury Lost Its Luster*. New York: Penguin Press, 2007.

Mark Tungate — *Fashion Brands: Branding Style from Armani to Zara*. Philadelphia, PA: Kogan Page, 2008.

Paco Underhill — *Call of the Mall: The Geography of Shopping*. New York: Simon & Schuster, 2004.

Thorstein Veblen — *The Theory of the Leisure Class*. New York: Oxford University Press, 2008.

Rob Walker — *Buying In: The Secret Dialogue Between What We Buy and Who We Are*. New York: Random House, 2008.

Sharon Zukin — *Point of Purchase: How Shopping Changed American Culture*. New York: Rutledge, 2005.

Index